7th GRADE READY

EXPERT ADVICE TO HELP PARENTS
NAVIGATE THE YEAR AHEAD

EDITED BY
TIMOTHY M. DOVE

A READY GUIDE

PARENT **READY**

PARENT READY.

2024-2025 Edition

Copyright © Parent Ready, Inc., 2024

Parent Ready supports the right to free expression and the value of copyright. The purpose of copyright is to encourage the creation of works that enrich our culture.

All rights reserved. No part of this book may be reprinted or reproduced in any form or by any electronic, mechanical, or other means, now known or hereafter invented, including photocopying, recording, and information storage and retrieval, without the prior written permission of the publisher, except in the case of brief quotations embodied in critical articles and reviews.

Published by Parent Ready
8 East Windsor Avenue
Alexandria, Virginia 22301
https://parentready.com

Parent Ready and design are trademarks of Parent Ready, Inc.

The publisher is not responsible for websites (or their contents) that are not owned by the publisher.

979-8-9880158-3-3 (paperback)
979-8-9880158-4-0 (e-book)

Bulk Purchases: Quantity discounts are available. Please make inquiries via https://schoolready.guide.

Table of Contents

Contributors vii

Preface xv

Introduction 1

Chapter 1: How Is 7th Grade Different from 6th Grade? 3
    Ways to support your child with teacher expectations
    Dylan Huisken, 2019 Montana Teacher of the Year

Chapter 2: How Is a 7th Grader Different than a 6th Grader? . . . 15
    An educator's perspective and advice for well-being
    Kristi Reinke, 2021 North Dakota Teacher of the Year

Chapter 3: New Morning Routines: New Building or Not 25
    How to set your child up for success in getting out the door
    Joy McKarns, 2021 Ohio District Teacher of the Year and
        State Finalist

Chapter 4: Dress, Lunch, and Fitting In 33
    A teacher's observations and checklist
    Joan Ebel, 2018 Nebraska Teacher of the Year finalist

Chapter 5: How Can I Help My Student Succeed
in the Classroom? 45
    Tips for encouraging your stressed-out student to stay
        on top of things
    Cindi Rigsbee, 2009 North Carolina Teacher of the Year

Chapter 6: Motivation and Overcoming Procrastination 57
    Teacher tips and tricks that might work at home too
    Stacey Donaldson, PhD, NBCT, 2010 Mississippi Teacher of the Year

Chapter 7: Overcoming Academic Setbacks 67
How to turn defeats into learning opportunities and build resiliency
Barbara J. Hopkins, PhD, 1988 Nebraska Teacher of the Year

Chapter 8: Different Learning Styles and Accommodations 79
How to support your child who is struggling in the classroom
Tyler Bartlett, 2015 Wyoming Teacher of the Year
Nikki Bartlett, 7th grade ELA teacher

Chapter 9: Challenging Student-Teacher Relationships 89
How to support your child if they aren't meshing with their teacher
Jamey Olney, 2000 DoDEA Teacher of the Year

Chapter 10: Constructive Parent-School Relationships 107
How can a parent best work with the school to support their student's achievement?
Angela Wilson, DoDEA 2012 National Finalist

Chapter 11: Online Daze 117
How can parents best support their virtual student?
Tom Jenkins, 2021 Ohio Teacher of the Year Finalist

Chapter 12: Out of School 131
What should a parent do if a child must miss school?
Erin McCarthy, 2020 Wisconsin Teacher of the Year

Chapter 13: Finding Passions in and out of School 141
How to discover and support your child's interests and activities
Meghan Everette, EdD, 2013 Alabama Teacher of the Year Finalist

Chapter 14: Are They Ready for 8th Grade? 153
Tips, Quips, and Tools
LéAnn Murphy Cassidy, 2018 Connecticut History Teacher of the Year and Connecticut Teacher of the Year Finalist

This series of books is dedicated to all those who contribute to the education and support of young people. I was lucky enough to be a classroom teacher for 32 years. I owe a lot of my effectiveness to those who worked with me and those who taught me so much over the years, especially two master educators, Jenelle and Mark Dove, my parents. We all have those teachers we think back on that made important contributions to our formal and informal education. Our parents and classroom teachers are on the front lines to encourage, question, teach, and celebrate us as individuals.

I want to thank all my colleagues who agreed to be a part of this project. We can always learn from one another if we are open to it. By having many voices in this conversation, we hope to be most useful to our readers in determining what would be most helpful in their own context. Thank you to all the educators who are still engaged in this sacred trust.

—Timothy M. Dove

Contributors

Editor

Timothy M. Dove, an educator for 42 years, is the Ohio State Teacher of the Year in 2011 and 2012. Tim was a middle school teacher for 32 years and helped develop the Global Scholars Diploma program. He taught high schoolers for three years, was an adjunct professor at The Ohio State University for 20 years, and for the past decade has worked with state and national education agencies supporting educators and students in a variety of ways. He has been a consultant with Battelle for Kids in Hong Kong, Learning Forward, the Council of Chief State School Officers (CCSSO), and the Collaboration for Effective Educator Development, Accountability, and Reform (CEEDAR) Center.

Contributors

Tyler Bartlett was selected as the 2015 Wyoming Teacher of the Year while teaching math and coaching at Newcastle Middle School in Newcastle, WY. He has been married to NMS 7th grade English teacher **Nikki Bartlett** for nine years. In 2019, Tyler became principal of NMS. Tyler and Nikki will pull this book off the shelf in years to come as their children, Lucy and Max, join them at the middle school.

LéAnn Murphy Cassidy, EdS, is the 2023 Smart/Maher VFW National Citizenship Education Teacher of the Year for the state of Connecticut, the 2018 Gilder Lehrman Connecticut History Teacher of the Year, as well as a 2018 Connecticut State Teacher of the Year Finalist. She is in her 35th year of teaching, serving simultaneously as a lead teacher and master mentor for the last 15 years. A member of the Connecticut Council for the Social Studies Board, LéAnn also serves on the Teacher Advisory Council for the National Constitution Center.

Stacey Donaldson is a 24-year educator and 2010 National State Teacher of the Year from Mississippi. Stacey is currently an assistant professor at Belhaven University and director of TESOL and ED Tech programs. Before joining Belhaven, Stacey started Learn Elation, LLC, supporting English language arts teachers, National Board candidates, and high school students. Stacey is an NBCT and certified in career and technical education. She has been involved in various aspects of mentoring and supporting teachers pursuing certification for the past 16 years. She earned a PhD in education from Walden University. She published her award-winning memoir *Psalm 23: Wonders of God's Love* in 2008. She's married to Johnny Donaldson, and they have two daughters, Camaryn and Cailyn.

Joan (Joni) Ebel has been teaching middle school students for more than 20 years in Nebraska and was Nebraska State Teacher of the Year finalist in 2018. She has extensive knowledge in teaching middle school mathematics and has served in various capacities for the state of Nebraska including in mathematics standards writing, college & career readiness standards, and on the Mathematics Content Advisory Board. She has been a finalist for the Presidential Award for Excellence in Mathematics and Science Teaching in 2019 and 2021. Teaching 7th grade mathematics is her passion, and she has served the students of Columbus Public Schools since 2001.

Meghan Everette, EdD, is currently serving as a full-time School Ambassador Fellow at the U.S. Department of Education. She is an elementary mathematics coach in Salt Lake City and the executive director of the ASCD Emerging Leader Alumni Affiliate. Meghan previously taught 1st, 3rd, and 4th grades and is proud to have taught at George Hall, the National Turnaround Model School. Meghan was the 2013 Alabama Elementary Teacher of the Year and a 2015–2017 Hope Street Group National Teacher Fellow. She co-designed Powered By Teach to Lead Utah and spent six years as a blogger for Scholastic, sharing classroom practices on everything from curriculum design to classroom libraries. She is the Utah ASCD president, has been a Digital Promise Micro-Credential Leader, and served on the CCSSO Teacher Recruitment and Retention Educator Steering Committee. Meghan co-authored *Forces of Influence: How Educators Can Leverage Relationships to Improve Practice* from ASCD. She received her doctorate from the University of Florida and her dissertation focused on how mass communication theory can be applied to improve school communication.

Barbara J. Hopkins, PhD, grew up in Nebraska and always knew she wanted to be a teacher. She taught English to middle school students in rural and urban schools, served as a reading specialist, and served as a school administrator who turned around schools that were challenged. The key for her, in education and life, is always showing you care and doing your best to help. Barbara is a Nebraska Teacher of the Year and the Nebraska Christa McAuliffe Award winner for courage in education. She and has been honored nationally with numerous other awards for her dedicated service. Middle school is her favorite grade span to teach because it sets the stage for students to succeed in high school and find the path to their future.

Dylan Huisken, Montana's 2019 Teacher of the Year, has served as a middle school social studies teacher for more than a decade, and currently works at a K–8 school in Bonner, Montana. He taught middle school in rural South Dakota before earning his master's in history at the University of Montana in Missoula.

Tom Jenkins, a seasoned educator for 26 years, has dedicated 24 years to teaching 8th-grade science, computer science, and STEM at Greenon Junior/Senior High School in Enon, Ohio. His accolades include Ohio State Teacher of the Year (District 10 & State Finalist), Air Force Association Ohio Teacher of the Year, and the Lemelson-MIT Excite Award. Leveraging his experiences as a NASA SOFIA Airborne Astronomy Ambassador and NOAA Teacher at Sea, Tom emphasizes data-driven critical thinking. His Greenon InvenTeam, supported by a Lemelson-MIT grant and Microsoft's #MakeWhatsNext, secured a patent for a pollution-prevention device. Tom has also served as a Teaching Fellow at Johns Hopkins Whiting School of Engineering and Lead Instructor at Air Camp. As a mentor, he's guided educators at Wittenberg University and the Dayton Regional STEM Center. He spent the 2022-2023 school year as an Albert Einstein Distinguished Educator Fellow in Washington DC. Currently, Tom serves as a Master Teacher of Invention Education with the United States Patent and Trademark Office, a Department of Defense STEM Ambassador, and a board member for Engineering and Science Foundation of Dayton Fund. He holds National Board Certification.

Erin McCarthy has guided children in exploring U.S. history as a social studies teacher for 13 years. After teaching 8th grade for 11 years at Greendale Middle School, she now teaches 7th and 8th grade social studies at the Indian Community School in Franklin, Wisconsin. Before she was a classroom teacher, Erin was an education manager at several midsize museums in the Chicago area. She managed school tours and programs but also mentored junior volunteers and interns. In 2022 Erin took a leave of absence to complete research in Greece as a Fulbright Distinguished Awards in Teaching Research grantee, researching how education ecosystems welcome groups who are often left out and create a sense of belonging. Her three children 18, 16, and 13, are thriving as explorers of the world.

Joy McKarns is the 2021 Ohio District 3 Teacher of the Year and state finalist for Ohio Teacher of the Year. Joy teaches 8th grade English language arts for Northmont Middle School in Clayton, OH. She is the 2020 Grand Prize Winner of the Henry Ford Innovative Teacher Awards. She received a 2022 Martha Holden Jennings Fellowship and led a team of teachers to El Salvador the summer of 2022. A National Board certified teacher, Joy has more than 30 years of teaching experience.

Jamey Olney teaches 7th and 8th grade English language development at Glick Middle School in Modesto, CA, where she serves as the English Language Development site coordinator and advises the Hispanic Youth Leadership Council. Jamey previously taught grades K–8 and has served as an instructional coach and school administrator in underserved communities throughout Northern California and for the Department of Defense Education Activity in Germany. She helped develop the National Board for Professional Teaching Standards Literacy: Reading-Language Arts certificate and was featured in the 2016 ASCD documentary *Disrupting Poverty*. In 2019–20 she served as a California Teach Plus Policy Fellow and is currently a Teach Plus Emergent Bilingual Change Agent Network leader. She was recognized as 2000 DoDEA Teacher of the Year, 2020 California League of Middle Schools Educator of the Year, and 2021 California Teacher Association School Bell award recipient.

Kristi Reinke is an 18-year veteran teacher (seven years in special education and 11 years in general education), with two years prior experience working in the school system as an education support professional (working with at-risk students). She has spent all but one of those teaching in a middle school in North Dakota. She holds a bachelor of science degree in criminal justice, a bachelor of science in education-social sciences/history and a master's degree in special education-strategist (supporting students who have learning disabilities, intellectual disabilities and autism, and emotional/behavioral disabilities) from Minot State University. Kristi had been involved in numerous professional activities, including school leadership, student council advisor, honor society advisor, Superintendent Advisory Committee, MPS district Safety Committee, executive officer of her local Education Association, and most recently she sits on the Teacher Cabinet for the ND State Superintendent. Kristi is the 2019–20 local Teacher of the Year, the 2020 County Teacher of the Year, and the 2021 North Dakota Teacher of the Year, and was awarded the North Dakota recipient of the 2022 California Casualty Awards for Teaching Excellence. She is married to Jason, a high school math teacher, and has college-age twin sons and a 14-year-old daughter.

Cindi Rigsbee has enjoyed over 34 years in education, most of that time in middle school classrooms. She has taught 6–8 English/language arts, worked on recruitment and retention efforts in individual school districts, and collaborated with teachers across North Carolina as a teacher on loan to the Department of Public Instruction. A National Board-Certified Teacher in the area of English/language arts, Cindi was named the North Carolina Teacher of the Year in 2009 and chosen as one of four finalists for National Teacher of the Year that same year. Currently, Cindi serves as a 7th grade English/Language

Arts teacher in a K–12 school. Her book, *Finding Mrs. Warnecke: The Difference Teachers Make*, was published by Jossey-Bass in 2010.

Angela Wilson is in her 22nd year of teaching. Fourteen of those years have been spent teaching middle school. Angela graduated from Western Illinois University with a major in elementary education. She received her master's degree from Southern Utah University. She's completed everything but her dissertation in reading literacy leadership. Angela is currently a 7th grade ELA teacher in Vicenza, Italy. Her students are children of U.S. military members. Angela was selected as the 2012 DoDEA Teacher of the Year and was one of the four finalists for National Teacher of the Year. Angela has also taught school in Illinois, Korea, and Turkey. She's held a lot of different roles, including staff development coach and literacy instructor. Angela has four beautiful daughters and is married to a talented middle school math and science teacher. When she's not planning tomorrow's lesson, she is traveling, chatting with her girls in college, and acting in theater productions.

Preface

When my wife and I had our first child, I remember looking at the little one in the hospital with both elation and dread. I was so excited to be a dad! Then it hit me. As a middle school teacher for six years, I have all this "education" and still had no idea what to do next. No directions. No manual. Our parents came to town for the birth, but after giving snippets of advice, they were on their way home.

Then some other thoughts hit me. We would get through this and do our best. And how awesome would it be when my daughter entered "my grade" as a 7th grader? This happened in the blink of an eye.

I remember vividly the days my daughter and son became 7th graders, because it was also my job, career, and calling. It is still amazing to me how two kids, raised in the same household with similar situations, can turn out to be so different.

There are many pivotal times in a person's life. Becoming a 7th grader is one of them. My wife shared with me the musings of Erma Bombeck as a backdrop of what was coming. She wrote about how your children, while in the early elementary years, are like puppy dogs. They come home still full of energy, happy to see you, and willing to share their experience of the entire day. Once they hit 7th grade, they tend to turn into big fat house cats. They "side eye" you and often show disdain for your shared wisdom. They will come eat when it suits them and rarely show any excitement in your presence.

Take heart. They do tend to turn into "adult dogs" in their early 20s, amazed about how you were able to do all the things you do and still raise the family. They do listen and watch. At the time, it may not seem so, but your words will come out of their mouths later (and it will drive them nuts).

Seventh grade is a time of a newly found idea of independence. This can drive you crazy. But, if the timing is right, this can be a time to begin adult conversations. These conversations will include subjects that matter in the long term. The timing of the conversations is often as important as the content. Look for the conversational opportunities and try not to miss them. It took me a while, but I learned that my best opportunity for meaningful conversations with my son was while I was driving him somewhere. I also discovered that asking questions was much more successful in facilitating conversation than telling him something. We still laugh today about paying attention to the road when we are talking, or we could look up and realize we are in another state.

A few conversational topics that have served my own (now adult children) well:

- Play "what happens next." Looking ahead at a choice of behavior or effort and how it affects not only you now, but in the future, is an important consideration. How the choice affects others is equally important. We don't live in a vacuum, although many 7th graders have not discovered that they are not the center of the universe...yet.

- Talk about how you might want to consider doing your best work the first time, on time. Rework due to lack of planning, effort, or thought is frustrating at best.

- Consider that not everything is as it appears. Many 7th graders (and some adults) don't have a larger view or context as to why things are happening the way they are. Help them find other adults who can help with this conversation. They are not always ready to hear it from you.

- Use the 24-hour rule. If something happens or is said that really pushes your buttons, it is usually better to let it sit for 24 hours before you say or do something you can't take back and regret. The time also allows a better planned response (if needed).

I want to invite you to enjoy the reflections and considerations shared by the contributors of this book. They are a wonderful collection of educators recognized at their state level for knowing a lot about education and middle school students. They also happen to be parents.

The message of this book is clear: Parents matter to a 7th grader. Just like 7th graders, parents come in many different forms. The bottom line is that they are individuals who love (if not always like) their children through it all. These students are improving their skills at problem-solving, understanding context, and manipulating their world both with positive and not-so-positive results. A parent's role to assist in the navigation of their children's growth and development as a person is paramount. Remember to find allies in other adults. Many times, I have given advice to my child that was ignored, but if the music teacher gave the same advice six months later, it was followed to the letter.

As a father of two and a career middle school teacher, I can tell you being the parent of a 7th grader is exciting, terrifying, frustrating, confusing, and joyous. Hopefully, you'll find some laughs and comfort in this book.

Timothy M. Dove
2011 & 2012 Ohio State Teacher of the Year

Introduction

This book is for parents, family members, caregivers, siblings, mentors, and any supporters of a soon-to-be 7th grader. Think of it as advice from the friendly teacher in your child's middle school.

Whether your child is entering middle school for the first time in 7th grade or has already spent a year there as a 6th grader, you'll find loads of information useful to you and your student.

Each contributor to *7th Grade Ready* is a current or former 7th grade teacher who has worked extensively with parents and families of students. These contributors have all been Teachers of the Year or finalists in their state. They are experts in the field overall and in the particular chapters they penned.

The chapters that follow cover many of the topics that you may be thinking about as your child enters 7th grade. Beginning with how 7th grade differs from 6th and moving through preparing them for 8th grade, this book will serve as your guide. It will describe what to expect in a variety of areas and things to look for as you navigate your child's physical, emotional, and academic growth.

This book focuses on both action items and tips on how to support your child as they start finding their independence. Some information might seem obvious, while other pieces will be eye-opening. Every family is different, and parts of the book will resonate differently with each reader. The new information can help you plan, and the things you already knew should assure you that you are on the right track. So, it could be read cover to cover, or by particular chapter of interest.

Most chapters conclude with a list of conversation starters. In thinking about how to use them, consider your relationship, family dynamics, and student's history. Using open-ended questions is the best way to get information from your student. Not only will having these conversations assist you in supporting your child, but they will also open new lines of communication that can continue throughout the school year.

Seventh grade can be a major year of change for your child. We hope this book helps you navigate it.

Chapter 1

HOW IS 7TH GRADE DIFFERENT FROM 6TH GRADE?

Ways to support your child with
teacher expectations

Dylan Huisken
2019 Montana Teacher of the Year

Middle school, with all its attending assumptions and cultural significance in our lives and our culture, is so named because it is, well, in the middle. And there is no middle school student more in the middle than the 7th grader. They are literally in the middle grade of many typical middle schools (6–8). Six years ago, a new 7th grader was learning to stand in a line. Six years from now, they will hopefully be lining up to ascend the graduation stage. A new 7th grader just two years ago was a 5th grader, and in two short years will be a freshman in high school. Navigating the long bridge of middle school toward the horizon of high school is challenging for all involved—the students, the parents, and the school staff—but to be smack dab in the middle requires some awareness of what has shifted since 6th grade. Indeed,

---

* We use the pronoun *they/them* in its singular form throughout the book because it is the most practical and inclusive approach.

7th grade is essentially a pivot point, a fulcrum that will accelerate them into their academic career, and ideally, a meaningful life.

Seventh grade differs from 6th grade significantly in a myriad of ways. This chapter is not about how 7th graders are different from 6th graders (for that, see Chapter 2). Rather, this chapter presents some ways that teacher expectations may shift after 6th grade, and it presents short sections on extracurriculars, organization, and philosophical outlooks. Most importantly, this chapter provides practical, healthy, and tangible ways for parents to support their students at home in a way that is aligned with the general goals of 7th grade teachers.

A Faster and More Independent Pace

A great deal of 6th grade instruction for 6–8 middle schools, especially at the beginning of the school year, deals with new routines, procedures, and spaces. From lockers and navigating different rooms with different teachers of different subjects, to learning organization skills in order to keep up with the ringing bells, 6th graders have a lot to learn in addition to the academic material. By 7th grade, teachers will assume that their students have had ample time to adjust to the rigors of a middle school schedule, which means things move at a faster pace. Early 6th grade lessons may include how to use a middle-school level textbook effectively, how to log into school technology or use a learning interface (e.g., Google Classroom), how to review a handbook or syllabus, how to respectfully communicate with classmates during group work, or how to meet behavior expectations and follow directions. By 7th grade, repeated and frequent early lessons on the skills of a middle school student or the structures of a school become less common, and expectations regarding behavior or independence are stated but not taught—in other words, teachers provide less guidance and fewer reminders. If your 7th grader is new to lockers or a multi-period schedule because they attend a junior high (grades 7–8) or are transitioning from homeschool, see the section in this chapter on organization (page 10). Whatever the case, the assumption is 7th graders should be decent self-starters, independent problem-solvers, and reliable managers of their own behavior in class.

So what does supporting your 7th grader at the beginning of the school year look like? Be sure to go over their schedule. If your child attended the same school last year, ask if they know where all their classes are, while looking at their schedule. Try to assess their familiarity with the teachers. Is it mostly the same teachers they had last year? All new teachers? What have they heard about them? Many districts, school buildings, and teachers have websites that share more about them and their expectations (and also provide staff email addresses). Once classes have started, read the syllabi or other materials provided by teachers and, if questions should arise, feel free to ask the teacher directly via email. This is a great opportunity for you to set the tone with your child's teachers: you are involved, curious, and communicative. After all, these are qualities we try to build in our students, and your outreach is in no way nettlesome or inconvenient. Other chapters in this book address morning routines (Chapter 3) and parent-teacher relationships (Chapter 10) in better detail.

If there is an online learning platform that students must use (e.g., Google Classroom), there are many YouTube videos on how parents can access their child's classes and keep an eye on their progress. Learn the online platform alongside your child. Invite them to show you their different classes and some of the materials they are covering in class. If you are unfamiliar with the school's online portal that allows you to check their grades, attendance, and tardiness, reach out to the school's counselors for help (also see Chapter 11 on technology). It will be especially helpful at the beginning of the year to see if your child is struggling to meet the pace of 7th grade, or to see if they are struggling to make it to class on time. If you notice a pattern in the first few weeks (e.g., being late for choir, which is at the other end of the building), it will be easier to brainstorm a solution for getting to class on time.

A Shift in Expectations: A Move to More Original and Abstract Thinking

All teachers want their students to grow into themselves, to find their voices, and to think in new and interesting ways. For 7th grade, the noticeable academic shift will be toward the more original and abstract thinking. Try to take notice at the start of the year, and as the year goes on, of ways that curricula or lessons may take on more difficult, abstract, original, student-led, or rigorous concepts. For example, my 6th graders study ancient history: they love learning about pyramids, the Great Wall, and the Colosseum. But by 7th grade, we are moving away from the "That's neat!" approach of studying history and more into the process of becoming a historian: critical analysis of difficult-to-read historical documents, theorizing on the mob mentality of witch hunts, studying current events in context, and doing the necessary work of learning about heavy topics like the Holocaust or the Crusades. My 6th graders learn about the events of the past and how to explain them with accurate facts and relevant vocabulary. By 7th grade, they start to learn how people interpret and record the events of the past to create historical narratives; they analyze and assess historical perspectives and try to synthesize conflicting records. In 6th grade, they read for details that support an idea they encounter in a book. In 7th grade they gather research in order to form and argue for their own original conclusions. In subjects other than history, teachers will also ask for original analysis: they will want your child to become a methodical scientist, an original and creative writer of many forms, a mathematician who understands the reasoning of concepts, a speaker of a new language—not just someone who can list some common nouns. Seventh grade will require more independent and original deep thinking, more deliberation, more effort, and the disintegration of the assumption that "finding the answer" is enough.

In most subjects, the ability to ask questions to lead to new insights is more important than "finding the right answer." In geography, a child could easily do an internet search to find out where India is, and memorize this for a quiz, like they would in my 6th grade class. But figuring out the right questions to understand what it is like to live in India requires a complex skill set. Encourage your child to be curious and to ask questions so they can take ownership of their learning. We want our students to be lifelong learners, so feel free to participate in your child's quest for new ideas, because then they will see you in this process. Model flexibility, open-mindedness, and curiosity. Try to avoid treating homework or other assignments as hoops that your child must jump through and instead as opportunities to practice new skills, ask authentic questions, and learn new concepts. Instead of asking, "What did you learn in school today?" which often invites a curt response or "answer," ask instead if they have questions about something that happened. This can be academic or not. Asking your child to reflect on the day, instead of spouting some rote fact, encourages authentic dialogue that won't come off like a status report. It invites new conclusions through thoughtful contemplation.

In tandem with the desire to help create lifelong learners, teachers want students to begin to develop their voices. We want our students to become advocates for themselves and others. We want them to sharpen their skills of communication and find effective ways to inform and express their opinions and passions. This often begins in earnest in 7th grade as one of the many ways for young teenagers to develop their independence. If your child comes home with a worry or concern about a teacher's expectation, ask if they have talked to that teacher yet. See what your child can do for themselves through self-advocacy before offering to reach out to a school staff member.

If you are concerned that there is too much "busy work" for your child to do every night, feel free to email the teacher and ask what the goal of the work is so you can support your child in attaining that goal. Is the goal to practice a new skill or to just "cover" a concept? Is it to work on reading independence or to build stamina for problem-solving? Teachers should be sharing their learning goals with students, and subject standards for your state are readily available through an internet search, but it is okay to ask teachers for a rationale so that you, as the parent, can have buy-in as well. When at parent-teacher conferences (which you should attend if able), don't ask about *how* your student is doing, for this invites a vague and perfunctory response. Ask instead about *what* they are learning; ask to see student projects, portfolios, or work; ask about upcoming units, tests, or long-term goals. This is not so you can grill your child every night over dinner about how they are progressing, but rather so you can be in the know and support your child from a healthy distance. It will be easier to invite discussion of new concepts or struggles if you are aware of some of the goals within your child's classrooms.

"Who Do You Want to Be When You Grow Up?" Not "What"

In a 2019 *New York Times* article, organizational psychologist Adam Grant encouraged parents to stop asking kids "what" they want to be when they grow up and ask them to reflect on what kind of person they want to be. Indeed, I despised this question as a middle school student, and I avoid it now as a middle school teacher. The abstract future is hard for the here-and-now mindset of a young teenager. Making goals because you've been put on the spot is hardly a method for deep thinking, and the question encourages a dismissive, one-word answer such as "veterinarian." Instead, try to get your child to wonder who they want to be when they grow up. Now, this may seem *more* abstract a question, and in many ways, it is. However, in

7th grade, it is an *actionable* question. Seventh graders can begin to wonder what qualities they would like to hone within themselves, that they could easily work on every day while at school in their routine interactions. Do they want to be seen as reliable, trustworthy, or loyal? Hard-working or resilient? Curious and open-minded? An advocate for justice, a good neighbor, a thoughtful friend, an involved community member? Seventh grade is a safe, pivotal time for them to begin reflecting on this. Next year they will likely be in the top grade of their school and will have to carry the weight of being a role model for the younger grades, whether they like it or not. By 9th grade, they will have to start off in a new environment, with graduation expectations looming. Seventh grade is the perfect time not to make post-diploma plans but rather aspirations for the kind of life they can lead through their everyday mindsets and choices, in both how they respond to injustices and how they move through their day. If they can practice this in 7th grade when the pressure is off to adapt to middle school (6th grade) or finish middle school (8th grade), then they can do this in life.

Middle school is often, and derisively, referred to as a time period that you simply must *survive*. I certainly viewed it this way as a tween. But 7th grade is the ideal middle ground where they can learn to warm up to new challenges, adjust to high expectations, and negotiate any peer drama that may arise. In other words, 7th grade can be the part of middle school where your child learns to *thrive*. The expectations may be higher in 7th grade, but the stakes are not. Failures or missed opportunities in 7th grade are not career ending. Seventh grade will come with its defeats and occasional failures, so help your child have the mindset that they are simply learning to step up at a place and time in their educational career where it is safe to slip up. Seventh grade is no time to fixate on GPAs or letter grades in unhealthy ways. Your child can certainly have goals related to these snapshots of progress, but *they are snapshots* that only capture a few insights about your child in one of the most important developmental time periods of their life. Help your child practice positive self-talk. Teachers know that 7th graders have a lot figured out but still have a lot *to* figure out, and that's an okay place to be.

A Quick Note on Extracurriculars and Sports

Seventh grade often becomes a time where participation in school extracurricular activities is encouraged or more attainable. Tryouts for a theater ensemble, sports team, spelling bee, or orchestra might be officially open for the first time, or perhaps more within reach. Perhaps this means your child will be an alternate, on junior varsity, or second chair, or perhaps this means they will begin their rise to a more advanced stage. If your school has an open house, attend it to see what is available. Consult the school handbook or find out which teachers also double as directors, coaches, and advisors to learn more. Ask about your child's interests and see what commitments from your own schedule you'll have to make to support their aspirations.

A Quick Note on Basic Organization

By now, your child probably has experience with a backpack, and maybe even a locker, but one thing to think about is how you can make sure these remain personal and powerful tools of organization. Ask if your child has any forms for you to sign or look over in the first days of school. Every so often, ask this question again and see if something from school is easy to locate in their backpack or not. Does your child rummage around for crumpled papers? That could be a sign that they are getting overwhelmed with the materials they think they need to do well in school. It is okay to ask your child what they need for each class and to find ways to reduce what is in their backpack. It is not unusual for a 7th grader to walk around with the extra weight of a graded project or an obsolete textbook for months on end.

Try to take notice when your child is not bringing home coats, lunch containers, gym clothes, or personal items. If not, they are probably in their locker. If a school allows kids to personalize their lockers, buying or borrowing locker shelves and fun magnets is an easy way for the locker to become a safe space. If the school uses combination locks, help teach your child how to use one in the early days of school (YouTube videos for this skill exist too!). If they use locks with a key, see if they can keep a spare key with the front school office (and try to have one yourself).

One tangible support for your child is to create a safe and calm study space where they can review notes, finish up assignments, or attend to homework. This is especially important as the rigor of school increases, as it does in 7th grade. If this is impossible or difficult to do, let the teachers know! Going back to self-advocacy, it is okay for students to make teachers aware of common home life situations, like familial obligations to watch younger siblings or no internet access. Some schools offer after-school library sessions or study halls. Some teachers allow students to work in their rooms before the bell rings to start the school day. Many teachers are willing to adjust expectations or brainstorm creative solutions.

In addition to finding spaces for your child to work in, however, encourage your child to read every night, even if it is for a short time like 10–20 minutes before bed. Above all, though, they should read with no agenda. No reading log to fill, no timer to tick, no questions to answer. They should read something they *want* to read, and not slog through something they think they have to or should read. Build in your child the desire to read for enjoyment. If this is something you want for your child, be caught in the act of reading for enjoyment around them as well. It could be your favorite magazine, a novel, a comic book, a food blog, or a collection of poems, but set the tone that something has now shifted. Look up from your book (or the article you're reading on your phone) and share something interesting that got you thinking. Because 7th grade is different—because the work will get more abstract, more difficult, and more time-consuming—it is important to form the habits of a curious learner and reader in order to make this transition organic rather than forced.

Closing Advice: Balance of Empowerment

Perhaps you have heard conversations in the media about helicopter parents who hover or lawnmower parents who remove all obstacles for their child. I refuse to lean on these tired stereotypes and instead invite you to figure out the best balance for supporting your child in ways that foster independence, allow them to learn hard but safe lessons through natural consequences, and empower them to practice self-advocacy, all with the safety net of your love and care below them. You should find ways to empower yourself as an ally to your child's 7th grade education, and I hope some of the advice in this chapter helps you get there.

Practicing how to support your child in 7th grade will better prepare them (and you) for their entrance into high school. Much of 7th grade is about empowering students with the skills that help them safely transition from 6th grade to 8th grade, so that they can enter high school with eyes wide open and adjust with flexibility. In 7th grade, high school is more of a distant horizon, visible but blurry. A good 7th grade education will help sharpen their eyes to the road ahead as they begin to spend more time in the driver's seat of their life. A decent driver knows the standard procedures of how to drive a car, and at one point has seen enough people in the passenger seat to help them, but this knowledge and support is not enough if they don't know where they are going or how to take heed of the warning signs and guidance ahead. Seventh grade should provide both the technical know-how of controlling their own progress forward and the mastery of how to navigate their inevitable stalls and roadblocks, and how to think through the yet unseen horizons beyond high school.

> **Conversation Starters**
>
> - Do you know where all your classes are?
> - Do you know any of your teachers, or what have you heard about them?
> - What parts of your new teachers' expectations cause you concern? Would you like to speak to them about these concerns?
> - Which class are you the most worried about? What is it about the subject, teacher-style, or class structure that concerns you?
> - How does 7th grade feel different than last year?
> - Do you have questions about anything that happened at school today?
> - *Who* do you want to be when you grow up? What qualities will help you get there?
> - What extracurricular activities might you be interested in pursuing this year?
> - What can we remove from your backpack that you don't need anymore?

Chapter 2

HOW IS A 7TH GRADER DIFFERENT THAN A 6TH GRADER?

An educator's perspective and advice for well-being

Kristi Reinke
2021 North Dakota Teacher of the Year

As a 16-year veteran middle school teacher, I tell my 7th grade students every year to be nice to their teachers because we really are a rare breed. Most middle school teachers I know are in it for the long haul, because in our eyes, 7th grade really is a hidden gem. I read a tweet the other day that said, "I just don't understand why anyone would actually WANT to teach middle school" and 33 middle school teachers responded with comments like, "we are a special kind of crazy"; "it's like going to a comedy show and boxing match at the same time every day"; and because you will see "some of the sweetness and eagerness of elementary but ready for deeper discussions and challenging tasks." I couldn't agree more!

I started teaching special education in middle school, but I have spent the last nine years teaching 7th grade and this is where I was meant to be. What I love most about 7th grade is that it really is that unusual stage when the students are too cool to ask for a hug but will gladly take one if you offer and when they will not volunteer to help but will happily stay after and help if you ask them to. I love being a 7th grade teacher. So much so that a student this fall even bought me a pair of socks that said: "Seventh Grader for Life!"—and she isn't wrong.

Puberty

From my perspective, the most obvious change you will potentially see in your child throughout their 7th grade year is puberty. I have more than 100 students a year. That means a student turns into a teenager almost every day of the school year—that's a lot of new hormones floating around. Almost every day, we sing "Happy Birthday" to someone and I say a silent prayer for their teachers and parents. There are the obvious physical changes you're going to start seeing in your child—their voice will be changing, they will start to break out, they will need to start using deodorant—and they might even start to form crushes on their peers. Some of them will need to start wearing bras and learn that the word "period" isn't something they should be embarrassed about. Fun fact, parents: most teachers have deodorant and extra pads and tampons (and some even have extra black leggings and shorts) in their desk drawers. Sometimes your kids ask us for these items because they are comfortable confiding in us on a topic that might not be discussed as much at home. Take this tip from a 7th grade teacher: use *puberty* as a common word in your house and once you normalize it, your child won't be so embarrassed about it.

Another physical change you'll probably notice in your 7th grader is their size. I'm 5'2". Most of my students show up on the first day and say, "I am almost as tall as you," and lots of them leave on the last day saying, "I'm taller than you." And if they aren't, they usually are by the time they leave 8th grade. Of course, this is the year that there seems to be vast size differences between kids. Some spend the entire year looking like they are barely in their double digits, and some appear to be in their full-fledged adult body. Besides infancy, 7th grade is the only time in someone's life that they go through so many physical changes—and they sneak up fast. (Side note to any parents whose child might be taking medication (particularly for attention deficit disorder): this growth spurt often changes how medicine is metabolized. A trip to the pediatrician and/or psychiatrist might be a good idea in the middle of the year to make sure that the dosage is still working for them. If you are unsure if it's still working, please reach out to the teachers, as we can definitely let you know if we've noticed any changes.)

New Experiences

Now that we have gotten the puberty talk out of the way, let's talk about how students truly blossom in 7th grade and seem to find their niche. The stereotypical 7th grade year is when students get glasses and braces and us oldies just talk about it being "their time to go through what we went through," but truthfully, it doesn't seem to be this way anymore. It seems that kids are getting braces and contacts in middle and upper elementary grades now and by the time 7th grade rolls around, they seem to be dealing with more mature situations. Gone are the days when all students come from a nuclear family. Every student that walks through the middle school doors has their own family dynamic and experience. Middle school is the time that some students are starting to figure out their gender and sexuality as well. Your child will come home and tell you about a peer they sat next to and how different they are from them. Embrace this conversation and enjoy the diversity your child is about to experience. Encourage them to be supportive of the differences, to make as many friends as they can, and to find those true friends that could potentially be in their lives forever. (Some of my best friends to this day were my friends in middle school and I *love* to share those stories and photos with my students so they understand how important true friends can be.)

Extracurricular Activities

One reason 7th grade is such an important year is because there are multiple extracurricular activities for students to be involved in. This is a year of experimenting and trying new activities and having a chance to meet peers that have similar interests. Even if you are in a school that does not offer many extracurriculars, your child will be exposed to new peers they might see out in the community engaging in similar interests.

Unfortunately, I've also seen students become overwhelmed with all these new choices. In elementary school, they are told what path to follow (class to lunch to library) while in middle school they are encouraged to try everything. Sometimes too many choices can feel overwhelming. I always try to take the time to get to know each student and help to direct them to activities that they maybe didn't even know they were interested in. When I see a student doodling, I mention art club. When I hear a student whistling or humming, I mention choir. When I see a student with fidgets, I direct them to the game club. Obviously, not all schools have all these options but there are opportunities for like-minded students to have the chance to get together outside of class.

Have you ever considered sharing your expertise as a parent? If so, contact your school; you never know if students want to be involved in a parent-led culinary class or foreign language course. In fact, I like to ask parents about their child's hobbies because you are the expert on your own child. Never feel shy about reaching out to your teachers to let us know about interests or hobbies your children might have outside of school so we can do our best to help them connect with others. I once had a young man in my class who was obsessed with trains and it turned out that a peer had *just* received a train set for a gift and didn't love it. I encouraged them to start chatting and next thing I knew, I had two young men in class who loved to share train stories.

Peer Opinions

Seventh grade is often the year that kids decide the opinions of their peers are way more important than the opinions of their family and teachers. (Teacher pleasing seems to be very important in elementary school, which is probably why some elementary teachers seem to need a U-Haul to bring home all their teacher appreciation gifts.) I have always said that 7th graders are like wolves: they like to travel in packs. There are natural born leaders and natural born followers. I feel that it's very important to find out which pack your child belongs to.

Obviously, teachers can't talk about other students, but we can share concerns about kids with whom your child is spending time, without naming names. Your child might come home and start talking about all the new people they are meeting, or they might decide they don't want their parents to know who they are associating with. As a teacher, I have a pretty good perspective on the students that are in my building so my own kids don't get away with much, but I am also the mom who is very involved in who belongs to my kids' packs. Do I know *everything* about everything going on in their lives? Absolutely not. But I can promise you that my kids know that they can talk to me about anything and that I will not place any judgment or criticize them for their questions and actions. Will I always agree with all of their actions? Again, definitely not, but making mistakes and facing consequences is a part of life.

Ask your 7th grader about their everyday activities and with whom they are associating. Ask your 7th grader's teachers if there are any social concerns you should be aware of. That does *not* automatically make you a helicopter parent. It shows your child (and their teachers) that you care about them. We will be honest with you because we want what is best for them. Sometimes you will find that they didn't turn in an assignment or are being habitually tardy because that is what helps them to fit in with their peers. And just because they don't want you to pack their lunch anymore doesn't mean they don't appreciate you offering; it just might not be what their tablemates are doing.

Gaining Independence

Another change you will probably see in 7th grade is your child walking the fine line of independence. Because they are sandwiched in between the coddling elementary years and the "now you are on your own" high school years, there is this need (from all perspectives—the students, parents, and teachers) for breaking out on their own. For example, in elementary school, if a child doesn't complete an assignment, the teacher will often make a phone call home or keep them after class to catch them up. In middle school, a teacher sometimes misses a missing assignment since we only see students for a 50-minute period. As we read in Chapter 1, 7th grade is sometimes the first time a student is going from class to class and has multiple core teachers. With this change, their responsibilities are much greater than they were during the previous seven years of school. They need to adjust to numerous teaching styles, different classroom setups, and multiple grading policies. This can be overwhelming for even a fully developed brain. By 7th grade, students are expected to be responsible for their own education (again, a lot of their teachers will have more than 100 students to keep track of on a daily basis). If they miss a day of school (and they will for many more reasons than being sick, as many extracurricular activities will take students out of class), they need to find out from the teacher what they missed (bonus if they get the work from the teacher *before* they miss the class so it is turned in and they don't get behind; see more on this in Chapter 12). Luckily, electronic communication is so easy via computer or phones and kids know how to use these devices better than we do! (Now if only someone could teach them not to write the entire email in the subject line or address their teachers as "yo" or "brah"—parents, I'm looking at you.)

Becoming Their Own Advocate

One true beauty that occurs in 7th grade is students find their voices. Finding this voice comes with a lot of responsibility. Advocating for themselves is not something students are often comfortable doing, particularly if they are at a new school with new teachers and new peers. Yet with seven years of formal education under their belt, *they* are the ones that know how they learn best. When I have a 7th grader stay after class and tell me that they need to fidget in order to concentrate, I find them a wobble stool or pedal desk. When they tell me that they are a visual learner, I make sure to get them a copy of the notes before we talk about them. When they tell me that they forgot to eat breakfast that morning and have a headache, I find a snack. This is what teachers do. But we aren't mind readers. We need students to tell us how they learn best. Please encourage your child to advocate for their needs.

Mistakes Are a Given

One last piece of advice that I can share: your 7th grader is going to make mistakes. They are going to do things that might land them in the principal's office, like constantly speaking out of turn, class clowning, or socializing at inappropriate times. The evening I was announced as Teacher of the Year in my school district, I ran into my 7th grade principal (who was also my PE teacher). The second thing he said to me—after "congratulations!"—was "do you remember when I had a desk in my office just for you?" and then he laughed. Truthfully, I don't remember that, and I think he was exaggerating a little bit, but I do remember getting in trouble and visiting his office on a few different occasions. Fast forward several years and not only am I doing pretty well in my adult life, I find that a lot of my "frequent fliers" to the principal's office end up just fine too, successful for the rest of their school career and beyond. So, if this happens to your child, don't automatically conclude that they are doomed. Let them learn from their mistakes and support them and the school's decision (i.e., a lunch or after-school detention) and you might actually find that these consequences makes them stronger.

Closing Advice

I recently found a diary from my mom (who passed away in 2017) that she kept when my sister and I were growing up. She mentioned numerous times how much she missed hanging out with us, how we never wanted to be home, and how much stress we put her through. When I did the math, it put me right around 7th grade. This was the time that all of the above-mentioned issues were so important to me (my peers, my social status, extracurriculars, fitting in, etc.) so I can see why she felt that way. As an adult, I had an amazing and trusting relationship with my mother so the fact that she never made me feel like I was doing something wrong back then must have worked. Now, as a mom of teenagers, I remind myself every day that just because they prefer to be with their friends, hide themselves in their rooms, roll their eyes whenever I want to have a discussion with them, or frequently give me one-word answers, it doesn't have anything to do with me. It comes with being "that age." My parents survived my 7th grade year, I survived my teenage boys' 7th grade years (although I did recently stumble upon a "teenager for sale" Facebook Memory that I wrote during that time), and I can promise that you, too, will survive your child's 7th grade year.

Conversation Starters

- Do you know if any of your friends have crushes yet? Do you talk about it amongst yourselves?

- Does the topic of "periods" come up at all? Do you know if you can ask your teacher for supplies?

- Have you met any new students who come from a different culture or background? Is there someone in particular you find really interesting?

- Are there students exploring their gender identity and do you have any questions about it?

- Do you think of your group of friends as leaders or followers?

- Do you feel comfortable reaching out to your teachers if you miss an assignment or if you need help understanding it? If not, why not?

- What do you think are the most common reasons for being sent to the principal's office? Do you think the consequences are fair?

Chapter 3
NEW MORNING ROUTINES: NEW BUILDING OR NOT

How to set your child up for success
in getting out the door

Joy McKarns
2021 Ohio District Teacher of the Year
and State Finalist

A morning routine; that's the dream! This idea is a no-brainer. Who wouldn't like a smooth, leisurely morning? Can such a thing exist with a middle schooler? We know that a morning routine can, first and foremost, ensure you won't be late. It also sets expectations, implements good habits for school, and encourages your student to respect time and set personal goals. It will also start the day with less stress, make it easier on parents—and who doesn't want less mayhem?

So why doesn't everyone have one? Because it takes the investment of time and persistence to create habits. It's work, but the work is up front, and the payoff is great.

The Morning Routine Starts the Night Before

The key to a morning routine is to decide on the most time-consuming tasks and do them the night before. By 7th grade, it's likely that you can no longer drop off forgotten instruments, lunches, or projects to school. So part of the routine is having your child start to remember all the things they need to take to school the next day. All of this takes discipline, but having a list will help.

- ☐ Charge electronic devices. One positive outcome of remote learning during COVID is that it provided students with the electronic devices they need to be successful. The only good iPad/Chromebook is a charged one, however. Be prepared to replace chargers, find your charger mysteriously missing, and listen to the accusation that your child's has been stolen. Do yourself a favor and keep the good one at home. Buy a drugstore charger to keep in the backpack.

- ☐ Plan outfits. This was a lot easier in elementary school. You will get the most resistance here, but this can be the biggest time-consumer in the morning. Don't do this for them, but give them all the choice in what they wear. Battle the clothes that don't meet dress code requirements at the store, not in the morning. Locate shoes. They will mysteriously creep away and end up in the weirdest places.

- ☐ Make sure alarms are set and set backup alarms. Every child awakes differently. Find what works best for yours. Some children need to eat right away. Others need extra time and several alarms to wake up. Maybe getting right in the shower works. Try different things.

- ☐ Shut off video games off at a pre-set time, NO MATTER WHAT. I believe this is the greatest cause of lack of sleep in teens, especially teen boys.
- ☐ Open, clean out, and pack backpack for the next day.
- ☐ Check agenda/calendar for any forgotten items, dress-up days, or assignments. Don't ask if your child has any homework in general; have them go through the mental list one class at a time. Compartmentalizing the day will help them focus and remember.
- ☐ Pack lunch or check that there is money on the lunch account. Fill up water bottle. If permitted, include a snack. Kids are hungry during the day before lunch.

Think of the to-do lists that run through your mind while you're trying to get to sleep. If you've taken care of it, it's off your plate and you're that much closer to a good night's sleep. The same goes for your child. The night-before preparations can feel overwhelming to do every night. I understand. Your child is putting one foot into the adult world. They may not know how to navigate it. Teaching them to be ready, less stressed, and on time can be some of the best lessons to prepare for adulthood. The more they do it, the easier and more routine it will become. This process is really about front-loading. Doing this routine together will eventually become a process that you must simply check on down the road, and by high school, a habit the child owns. Invest this time now as it will pay dividends in the long run.

Phones

I highly recommend that a middle schooler's phone is charged at night away from them, in your kitchen or your bedroom. You'll hear every plea in the world, but giving them a break from social media drama will help them sleep and focus on getting ready for school. I wouldn't hand over the phone until they are completely ready to walk out the door. If you drive them to school, it should be the last thing they get before they open the car door at school. Enjoy any talk you can encourage out of them on the ride. If they have their phone, their focus will be on the social media drama of the evening before all the way to school and they will start their day drenched in drama. Kids truly need this break from social media.

When Should the Alarm Go Off?

This is a burning question. What time do we set those alarms, for both you and your child? You may have to keep adjusting the alarm time, depending if you and your child are able to get out of bed with the alarm. Not everybody can. Whatever amount of time you need, *add 20 minutes*. You will always use the time: forgotten homework, a pit stop at the store to grab a poster board, a broken zipper—it's inevitable, it will happen, and that time cushion will save you every time. Worse case, nothing happens and there's time to relax. What better way to start the day?

Breakfast

Don't skip this: plan for it. You don't have to be Martha Stewart and get the eggs from the chicken out back to start them off right. Don't let them start their day with a sugary breakfast. I can tell by second period which students ate protein, which students ate sugar, and which students had no breakfast at all. Heads go down, eyes glaze over, and no learning is going on. Giving your child the advantage of a quick egg and sausage sandwich, peanut butter on toast, or bacon or cheese on a bagel will set them up for success. Find what they like; they'll happily eat it every day.

Energy Drinks

Once you've watched a middle school student convulse on the floor in the midst of a grand mal seizure from an energy drink, you'll never see the vast cool factor that these kids see in these drinks again. In fact, after the second time watching a student seize and fall to the floor, I view these drinks as poison and fear grips me when a student walks in my room holding one. Just Google "dangers of energy drinks and kids." I know the confidence a drink can impart when placed in the hand of a 7th grader upon entrance to the school. They wave this badge of adulthood around like a royal scepter. I found a compromise with my own middle school children. We had the advantage of riding together to and from school each day. If we were able to leave the house on time, we would stop at whatever gas-n-go stop was on the way and they would carefully prepare a one-quarter cup coffee with three-quarters of hot chocolate in a standard coffee cup. *Voila!* Enter a confident and only mildly caffeinated middle school student to rule the school that day.

Morning Hygiene

Don't assume your middle schooler has mastered good hygiene. Just because they get in the shower doesn't mean soap is being used. Be observant and offer all the deodorant and body wash they can use. Be careful not to nag, criticize, or pester them. They will not dress to your standards. They are stretching, experimenting, exploring who they are and expressing this in their clothing. Just make sure the clothes and body are clean. Be encouraging, maybe excited about a new fragrance you found, or kindly suggest a shower, but don't dwell on greasy hair. More important than supplying them with gum is to make sure teeth are getting brushed. Designer clothes and the right shoes mean very little when basic hygiene is not being met.

The Bus

The school district will send you the bus stop location, time of pick up and drop off, and bus number before the first day of school. Encourage your student to develop a relationship with the driver. They should greet them when they get on the bus, be helpful, follow rules, and be kind to others on the bus. The ride can be a vulnerable time for kids. Encourage them to remove themselves from situations that aren't appropriate and not to be afraid to ask the driver for a new seat.

Check In at the End of the Week

What did they do right in the morning? What did they do wrong? Ask these important questions, brainstorm some suggestions together, and set them up for a good next week. You might be surprised at what really helped them and what didn't.

Set Them up for Success: Attitude

Did I say *attitude*? No one can give you attitude like your middle schooler. So, drop all your hurt feelings, and don't take it personally. **The most important thing you can do to help your child be successful is to start the day with a positive attitude.** If they pick a fight with you, shrug and listen. If they dump all their anxiety on you before they head out the door, be glad they left it at home and didn't take it with them to school. If they leave in tears and offer no explanation, you will feel helpless but know that if you offered love and encouragement even though you couldn't fix it, you created a safe space for them to come home to. So put on that insult-proof armor, thick skin, and reactionless face. Smile, encourage, and just be present. That will be enough.

Closing Advice

Remember that your job is not to fix the problems. You can listen, advise, and encourage but the fix should be with your child. If they forgot an assignment, have them contact the teacher. If another child has been cruel, try to let them handle it. Don't swoop in unless absolutely necessary. The more problems they solve for themselves, the better they equip themselves to handle adult situations as they come along in life. Celebrate victories, console defeat. There is nothing a Cherry Limeade from Sonic can't make a little better. I found that sitting in the drive-through lane with my child after school gave them some time to vent, unwind, and get some perspective. Just listening can be the very best tool in your parenting tool belt.

And speaking of belts, get ready to fasten your seatbelt. This doesn't have to be a bumpy ride. In fact, this can be quite a joyful ride. Remember to laugh, to learn, and let them lean on you.

Conversation Starters

- Is your Chromebook plugged in?
- Have you checked your schedule to see if there is a special school day this week? If so, what is it?
- What projects are due in the next week or so? What tests are coming up?
- Is your outfit laid out for tomorrow? Including your shoes?
- Is your backpack ready to go?
- Have you filled up your water bottle? Do you want a packed lunch tomorrow?

- Do you need money in your school lunch account?
- Will you shower tonight or tomorrow morning?

Chapter 4
DRESS, LUNCH, AND FITTING IN

A teacher's observations and checklist

Joan Ebel
2018 Nebraska Teacher of the Year finalist

Let's face it, 7th graders can have an aroma! Adolescence is a time of change, the biggest since they were between the ages of birth and three. That baby now has smelly feet and things are growing... their feet, height, body hair, body parts, and attitude. This phase will pass, but it can be a trying time for any adult who encounters a 7th grade adolescent creature. They can also seem like Dr. Jekyll and Mr. Hyde—one minute they are the sweet, loving child you raised, who hugs you and says they love you, and the next minute they have purple hair, randomly walk into things, touch *everything* (physical objects *and* each other), have a language all their own, and, on top of all that, own an attitude. You wonder what you created, how you will get through the next emotional tirade, and if this roller coaster will ever end. Yes, it will! You will live through it, and they will too.

Dress

To navigate the murky waters of 7th grade clothing styles, just watch any Netflix/cable/YouTube channel or social media app your tween/teenager watches—but watch in *secret*, as they will absolutely *die* if they find out you are watching the same content as they are! Beware: along with body changes, their viewpoint regarding their clothing changes just as fast as their attitude. That great-looking hoodie they received for their birthday and wore for three straight days will all of the sudden be (a) the grossest thing they ever saw and/or (b) not fit because they went through a growth spurt overnight. Watch this especially with girls' clothing; what might have fit one or two months, or even weeks, ago is suddenly too tight.

You can also scan through any teen-focused magazine in your grocery store to see the latest trends in fashion. Again, your teenager will roll their eyes and then swear they will "die" if they see you doing this. They will live. Use the internet to peruse and research online trends too. Teenagers tend to want to dress like their friends (and this is where most of their influence comes from) and also their favorite influencer, which can be expensive! Have your teenager show you what clothing trends or ideas they like.

On the flip side, your tween/teenager may wear the same clothes day after day after day. Remember that hoodie they received for their birthday? It still fits and here it is, every day! It's comfortable and even though it's been worn for four days in a row, and even though it's piled in a heap on their floor, it's still clean, right? Teenagers want to be "invisibly seen." This means they really don't want other people to be looking at them, although they think or believe that *everyone* on planet Earth is looking at them. Yet they want to be seen and recognized, maybe for something they do or say. Maybe they want to be seen and recognized for their clothing choices or style. They don't want to be embarrassed. Since teenagers want to be "invisibly seen," wearing the same thing day after day can draw attention and comments from peers about how they "smell," even if they don't. Have those clothing items been washed even though they wear them constantly? Comments may come regarding whether the student can afford other clothing. This can be traumatic to 7th graders (or any middle school–aged student). They want to be accepted, not degraded for something so trivial. And 7th graders can make pretty much anything trivial!

Hygiene

Smelliness and hygiene go together. Invest in deodorant, stick or spray. Your child's teachers will thank you! Imagine the following scenario: you haul them off to school, where they join other potentially aromatic students, let's say 20 to 30 of them, in a confined classroom that may or may not have windows. If those windows exist, they may or may not open to circulate air. Then they go to fitness or P.E. class, run (literally!) around in the same clothes they are wearing (or they may change into fitness clothes that haven't been washed in a few weeks.. because they forgot to bring them home!), and they get sweaty. This group of 20 to 30 teenage creatures then return to the same confined classroom with limited air circulation. Let the fermenting begin! Buy deodorant and teach them to use it *often*.

The converse of this are those students who go overboard with the cologne/perfume/body spray and stop at their locker after every single class and spritz until a fine fog of pleasant-smelling aroma surrounds them. And then they go to class. Imagine the laundry and candle aisles of your grocery/department store *combined*. Yes, it's like that for a teacher...for eight hours every day, especially in the spring. (More on that later.) Although we appreciate their consideration (let's face it, they are trying to impress others), they do go a little overboard on the spritzing. Teach your teenager that less is often more and that using cologne/perfume/body spray is not equivalent to using deodorant.

Make sure they are showering. As adults, we know how important it is to have a schedule: waking up, working out, showering, getting dressed, and arriving at work on time. Then we must get our teenager to do the same. Sometimes showering or bathing can get forgotten due to time constraints (they need *a lot* of sleep; this is normal!). They may even argue with you and make statements such as, "I will shower later," "I took a shower yesterday," or "I showered this morning" and then the shower/bath never happens. Students can show up to school not having bathed or even combed their hair for days at a time. Remember, they want to be "invisibly seen." But this habit will no doubt get them seen and talked about by their peers if it happens more often than not. Follow a schedule (see Chapter 3), get them up, get them in the shower, feed them breakfast (some schools offer breakfast on site), and get them to school.

Seasonal Dress

Seasonal dress is a "thing" with 7th graders as well. After teaching for 20-plus years, I've noticed a few things that are the same year after year. First, shorts. You will see 7th graders wear shorts year-round, no matter what area of the country you live in, and no matter the outside temperature. It could be 30-below and there will be 7th graders who wear shorts daily. Sometimes they don't realize that the outside temperature is not the same as their home's temperature, or that the outside temperature is not controlled by their parents. They arrive at school, survive half a day in school being "okay" and say, "I'm fine" when asked if they are cold. Then they call home and want their hard-at-work parent(s) to bring them warmer clothes. The same could be said about wearing a t-shirt. Seventh graders don't think about the temperature—they are too concerned about other areas of their life to take "outside forces" into account. Their world exists right in front of their face and nowhere else. None of this is a big deal, just an observation.

Secondly, no coats. The "I'm fine" comment you will hear from your 7th grader, no matter what question you ask them, is common when you ask them to put on a coat or jacket when the temperatures dip lower. They go from home to bus/car, to school, to home (with other activities in between), and often choose not to wear a coat. If they walk to school, they may even choose to not wear a coat during this time as well. This is a head-shaking time for us adults. Pick your battles. Do they really need one? What life lesson will they learn by not wearing one? But be ready for the moment you get in the car and they realize they want a coat. They may not say anything, as they don't want to be embarrassed by being "wrong" when you had just suggested moments ago that they put on a coat. They will respond with "I'm fine" once again because you asked them for the sixth time that morning if they want their coat. But they may actually say something about wanting to go get their coat. Do not be judgmental here and say something like, "I told you this already! Hurry up, we are late!" Just let them go. It's what you wanted them to do all along and they made the choice you wanted…just later than what you wanted. But they made the right choice!

Finally, springtime. Spring is a time when the weather begins to warm up, things are turning green, and 7th graders realize they are closer to 8th grade (and high school) than ever. They begin to want to attract the attention of other teenagers, and their wardrobe shows it. This is often a time when questionable, or more "revealing," clothing choices come into play, particularly among the female student population. And what they walk out of the house in that morning may or may not be what they arrive home in that evening. Remember earlier when I mentioned that they touch everything? They also are known to trade clothing with each other: shoes, shirts, shorts, etc. You may not approve of something your child wants to wear, but their BFF's (Best Friend Forever) parents do not care. (Or the BFF's parents *do* care, but teenagers can be sneaky. They could have earned and/or saved up money and then bought an article of clothing their parent(s) would not approve of and without their knowledge. Even though they might tell another adult their parents approved or said it was okay, the parents might not even know.) So, the BFF brings the article of clothing to school and lets your child wear it. Your child comes home dressed differently and you wonder if you are "losing it." Watch what happens when springtime rolls around. It's eye-opening, to say the least. Your teenager is growing up!

A Handy Checklist

To help wrap up this section on dress, here's a quick checklist to help:

- ☐ Deodorant
- ☐ Deodorant
- ☐ Deodorant
- ☐ Shower or bathe
- ☐ Brush teeth
- ☐ Comb or brush hair
- ☐ Clothing that fits
- ☐ Clothing that is clean
- ☐ For females: bras, underwear, socks
- ☐ For males: underwear, socks
- ☐ Look at trends for middle schoolers online, in magazines, and on shows

Lunch

Inner dialogue of a middle schooler at lunch:

"Where do I go? Where do I sit? Who do I sit with?"

What do I eat? Do I even eat? Do I have enough time to eat?

I don't like the food, it's gross. Oh, I like that food.

Where's my friend? Who can I talk to? I'm going to get lost. I am lost.

How do I carry this plate/tray and walk and talk to my friend at the same time?

Is that my friend over there? If I walk over there to see my friend, everyone is going to stare at me walking. OMG, they are all staring at me!

I'm going to cry. They are going to stare at me because I'm crying.

I don't have anyone to sit with. I will just sit by myself. But, if I sit by myself, they will stare at me. I'm all alone. I don't have time to eat!"

Lunch can be a stressful time for students. It's one of the instances during the day where time isn't as structured as during their classes and this can cause anxiety. If your student is brand new to a school, the best advice I can give is to get them into the building prior to their start date. Take a tour or attend a sporting event and let them get their bearings. Sometimes the cafeteria is also the concession stand area for athletic events and attending an event can familiarize your teenager with the layout.

When researching this topic, I asked several middle school students from a variety of school settings what they "do" for lunch. What recommendations would they have for a new student to help them out? The following are some of their responses:

- Try all of the food to find out what you like and then try to sit with people you like talking to.

- Sit by people you think would be friendly and open to being friends with you.
- Find yourself a good set of friends. Make sure they understand each other and know how to get along, with a small amount of teasing here and there.

The resonating theme in their comments is to find friends or people you enjoy talking to. Students can always ask a teacher or other adult for help too. Most school cafeterias have protocols or rules (see list below) in place for students to follow during lunchtime. Your child will figure it out. Having friends to talk to and assist in this transition is most helpful.

Protocols for lunch—this can vary depending on your school's size and location:

- How to enter and exit the cafeteria.
- Where to sit (perhaps they sit as a class group or in a certain area of the cafeteria).
- How to talk (not yell) when you are in the cafeteria.
- Where to line up to receive your lunch.
- Not to throw food or other items (yes, teenagers "forget" this).
- The number of students who can be in a particular line.
- How to greet or talk to the cafeteria workers (politely; remember your manners!).
- How to clean or put away your dirty tray and silverware.
- How to clean up the area around where you were sitting.

Fitting In

As adults, we might remember the friends we had during our middle school years. We might even still have some of those friends. We might also remember the cliques and drama that occurred during this time. How did we fit in? In some respects, this process hasn't changed. And in other aspects, it has drastically changed! The internet, social media, and the fact our teenagers are constantly "plugged-in" to something is radically different from how our generation was raised.

I asked some middle school students from different schools and different grade levels what their thoughts were regarding "fitting in" to 7th grade and what advice they would give to either a middle school student who they knew or a new student to their school. Here are their responses:

- Don't fake your personality.
- I would just be yourself and be kind and positive.
- I would tell them not to do anything they don't want to do and focus and work.
- Stand out and introduce yourself to people; reach out and make friends.
- Find people you like and become friends with them.
- Make friends in every class you have; you have different people in each class.
- Be kind and nice to people.
- Wear a hoodie and shorts.
- Well, they don't need to fit in, they need to be themselves, but [the way] to do well is to listen and make friends.
- Be yourself, find your people.

- Surround yourself with good friends and then you're basically good.
- Do what you want (what interests you) and you will fit into where you want to be.

The resonating theme in their comments is to "be yourself," be kind, and you will find friends or people you enjoy being around.

Closing Advice

Seventh graders need to be reassured you will always be there for them. As they start to experiment with various hair colors and clothing styles, they want to be reassured (not necessarily verbally) you will be accepting of the wild and crazy things they do. Sometimes this can lead to experimenting with risky behaviors. Set appropriate rules (yes, they will see this as the *end of their life!*) and keep the door open for discussions. *Listen* to what they say: don't listen to respond, but listen for the underlying (coded) message they are trying to convey to you. They don't necessarily come right out and say what they want to say, and that's okay. You must learn to "speak teen" and that can be a scary language to navigate! There is eye rolling and saying, "I know" and "I'm fine" *a lot*, but they are listening. Make sure you are informed as well—from their clothing styles, friends, and apps on their phone to the words they say…EVERYTHING. Often what they say is "coded." Try to keep yourself in the know.

Conversation Starters

- Tell me about Netflix/YouTube/cable shows' characters whose sense of style you like.
- Which are your favorite sweatshirts to wear?

- Do you have deodorant at school that you can use after gym class?
- How is the food in the school cafeteria? What is your favorite meal? What meal isn't so popular with your friends? Do you have enough time to eat?
- What did you eat today? Did you swap with any friends or get something from the cafeteria?
- Have you found a good crew to sit with during lunch? What do you like talking about?
- Who are your friends in each of your classes?
- Do you feel like you can be yourself in school? Why or why not?

Chapter 5

HOW CAN I HELP MY STUDENT SUCCEED IN THE CLASSROOM?

Tips for encouraging your stressed-out student to stay on top of things

Cindi Rigsbee
2009 North Carolina Teacher of the Year

"Elementary students are to caterpillars as high school students are to butterflies. Therefore, high schoolers are to butterflies as middle schoolers are to _____.

Answer: Howler monkeys. That's right. Sometime between caterpillars and butterflies, the human child becomes an entirely different species." —Heather Wolpert-Gawron, *Tween Crayons and Curfews: Tips for the Middle School Teacher*

Who Are They?

During my years as a 7th grade English/language arts teacher, I began the school year with the following quote from *Alice's Adventures in Wonderland*:

"Who are you?" said the Caterpillar. This was not an encouraging opening for a conversation. Alice replied, rather shyly, "I—I hardly know, Sir, just at present—at least I know who I was when I got up this morning, but I think I must have been changed several times since then."

This quote sat atop my syllabus and was part of my room decor because it encompasses all things 7th grade. I may see a child enter the room, become a completely different student later in the class period, and yet another version walking into the hallway for their next class.

There's a reason Gary Soto wrote a book entitled *Seventh Grade*. And there are other titles: *Seventh Grade vs. the Galaxy* by Joshua S. Levy, *Seventh Grade Weirdo* by Lee Wardlaw, and *My Life in the Seventh Grade* by Mark Geller, to name a few. These authors are onto something that teachers have known for a long time: 7th grade is a special year in the life of a preteen, the year that your precious smiling child may be first overtaken by teen angst and social drama. "Hormones on skateboards," I've called them.

In my experience, 7th grade is the year parents may first become concerned about a child who has never had problems in school before. I have held many parent-teacher conferences with tearful moms saying, "But he wasn't like this in elementary school. I don't know what to do." As the years went on, I became more experienced and eventually had the opportunity to "encourage" my own children through 7th grade. Those experiences enabled me to help stressed-out middle schoolers—and their parents— navigate through the obstacles they faced during that very important year.

Communication

Throughout my 30-year teaching career, I have had the honor of helping two different junior highs transition to the middle school concept. Prior to the opening of 6–8 grade middle schools in the early '90s, junior high schools held grades 7–9. Seventh graders were the rookies who had just left the elementary school, where they were BM/WOC (big men/women on campus).

Parental concern over lack of communication from the school was prevalent during those years. Gone were the weekly folders sent home by elementary teachers and the frequent phone calls made by teachers who had a class of 29 (as opposed to junior high classes of four periods times 29 students each). Seventh grade is the year when students often stop relaying information to their parents. Letters home sit in the abyss of their backpacks, progress reports go unsigned, and report cards can bring surprises to parents who remember their elementary children running through the door, waving returned papers at them.

As those junior highs became middle schools, and technology became more commonplace, it became easier for parents to stay on top of their children's school life and happenings. Here are some common ways to do so:

School Websites

I have never clicked on a school website that didn't include a school calendar on it. You can find information about the dates for spring break and the day the progress report will come home. There are school-supply lists, teacher bios and web pages, and links to online learning resources. There is school news that can serve as conversation starters with the middle school child who has clammed up (after all those elementary years of babbling on and on in the carpool line.)

Click often for updates and keep a lookout for important announcements that will keep you in the know.

Grade Portal

Speaking of online: if you had told me when I started teaching that assignments and grades would be available to parents 24 hours a day, I would've done a cartwheel. I currently check my middle school granddaughter's grades daily (more often if she's taking a test that day), and I'm able to intervene if I notice a problem. Our current culture of grades is one of transparency. Teachers want parents to know that we are working together as a team for the success of the students.

Email

My son was in middle school when teachers were first trained on how to use email. It was magical! I remember his math teacher sending an email during homecoming week, outlining spirit days. My son hadn't mentioned it, but once I brought it up, he was ready to participate. If parents have questions about classwork or an upcoming test, email is the way to go. It's difficult to get teachers on the phone when they are standing in front of a classroom full of students. Email is more practical and can provide quick answers to most questions. Most teachers share their email addresses on back-to-school night, and you can usually find them on the school's website as well.

Phone Calls/Conferences

Communication that requires more time, or that is more sensitive, may necessitate a phone call. But starting with an email to schedule the call will save time and voicemails (aka phone tag). Sometimes a face-to-face conference is needed just to ensure that everything is being communicated in a positive way. When I started out as a teacher, I didn't recognize the power of those meetings, but later it became apparent. When all in attendance have the best interest of the student in mind, goals can be set for student success, and parents and teachers can work together to ensure that success.

Study Skills and Homework

Structure and scheduling are two of the biggest contributors to student success in studying and completing homework. Middle school students haven't developed strong organizational skills yet, and middle school teachers work hard to establish those habits. My job as a middle school teacher is to prepare students for high school by teaching them how to organize classwork, notes, binders, lockers, and backpacks. But these skills aren't only needed at school. Parents can be an integral part in ensuring that students are prepared for the pressures of classwork, homework, quizzes, and tests.

Time

Over the years, parents have asked me to recommend a study schedule so students can organize their home study time. Here's an example:

3:30—home from school/snack

4:00—homework/study

5:15—activity/outside time

6:00—dinner/clean up

7:00—bath/clothes out for next day (backpack packed up)

7:45—read/bedtime (depending on age)

This schedule is ideal, of course, and doesn't take after-school programs, ball games, and other extracurricular activities into account. Luckily, most after-school programs incorporate homework time, but other activities can throw a schedule off. My granddaughter, who is a middle school cheerleader and softball player, has many nights when she gets home at almost 9 p.m. On game days, she has to use her class time wisely, working on homework during any time available during the day, and then looking it over or finishing it up at night. Luckily, she has one teacher who doesn't assign homework on school game nights. That helps some, but of course there are many students who have activities at night that aren't related to school (church, scouts, recreational teams) so it's important to be creative to be sure students have time to complete work.

It's important to have a schedule in place even if situations (like extracurriculars) call for modifications. In my experience, children who adhere to a schedule have easier days at school and sleep better at night. The name of the game is structure; it works for adults, and it works for kids. Creating a schedule and sticking to it (as much as possible) can make a big difference in school success.

Space

Even if a desk in an isolated spot in the house isn't available, determine a study space that works best for your child. The kitchen table can work if it's not during the hustle and bustle of meal preparation. The sofa in the den works if the television is off. And these days, we have to explicitly say, "phones down." It's a wonder today's children can get anything done with those "distraction devices" everywhere. (I speak from experience—social media seems to call me the loudest when I'm the busiest!)

Some students, especially those in higher grades, like to do work in their bedrooms. It's important to consider the study behaviors of each individual child to determine if that's an option. Research indicates that doing homework in bed is not the best practice for obvious reasons. Beds are for sleeping, so working there can reduce focus.

Also, it's difficult to organize papers, books, and laptops in the soft, warm folds of your bed. It's better to reserve the bed for sleeping and find an alternative study space.

Falling Behind/Learning Challenges

As a teacher, my first move when a student's grade starts falling is to contact the parents. As a parent, my first instinct is to reach out to the teacher. If you notice a dip in grades or if you see missing assignments on the grade portal (or progress report, etc.), the first thing to do is talk to the teacher (after getting your child's perspective, of course). That's why it's important to be diligent about keeping an eye on the grade portal so there are no surprises (and so it's not too late to turn things around once problems begin). Communication with the teacher is essential in order to determine the root of the problem (i.e., missing work, work turned in late, low test scores, or other issues that can impact success in the classroom).

I once had a student who kept falling asleep in class. My efforts to keep him awake weren't working, so I called the parents. After some investigation it was determined that the child was up all hours of the night playing video games. Unfortunately, this isn't surprising these days, and kids are sneaky under the cloak of night when parents are asleep. But without that communication, this behavior could have had a dire impact on grades and learning.

Here are some steps for helping a student who is struggling in school:

1. Communicate with the teacher. You need to have all points of view, not just your child's. I can't tell you how many times students have talked to me about difficulties in another class and said, "The teacher doesn't teach us anything. I've asked for help but he won't help me." These types of "misunderstandings" are

common and definitely need to be addressed with a face-to-face meeting, with all parties respectful and listening.

2. Note: A wise colleague of mine used to remind me, "Perception is reality." It may not be the teacher's intention to be unwilling to help a student or to even be demeaning or critical, but if the student feels that way, it's valid and can impact learning. That's why communication is so important. Then if you, as a parent, have concerns about a teacher, it's appropriate to talk to an administrator. But as an educator, I'd ask you to talk to the teacher first. Many miscommunications can be handled at the parent-teacher level.

3. Make a plan with the teacher. Some students may need a daily planner to go home for a parent signature. This planner can include assignments due, any behavioral concerns to be noted, and any other vital communication. Other situations may call for a redesign of the study schedule if it's not working. But it's important to leave the parent-teacher meeting with a plan to help the student turn things around.

4. Bring others into the conversation. If meeting with the teacher and making a success plan doesn't help, the school guidance counselor can be helpful. Sometimes, administrators need to become involved, too. They may suggest that the student complete some assessments that will explain (or alleviate) any concerns about learning behaviors.

5. Bring in extra support if needed. Communicate with staff in the special education department of the school if it is determined that a student may require modifications and learning support. And continuing to communicate with the regular education staff is an important part of the student's support system.

6. Set up for success. Even if no learning problems are identified, the planner mentioned above, daily grade checks, and monitoring distractions like phones and video games can help a student with focus and work ethic. And again, structure and schedules are the name of the game when students are at home.

Staying Connected with Your Child

I have witnessed (and even felt) the heartbreak that occurs when our children are suddenly "tweenagers with an attitude." The hugs that used to be commonplace seem to be buried underneath snide remarks and rolled eyes.

Recently, I talked with two 7th grade girls about communication with their parents. They both said, almost in unison, "We don't tell them anything... because they don't understand." They shared some more sentiments: *school is different now, they don't even teach math the way they did when my parents were in school, I'm lazy and I don't want to get fussed at for not doing my best....so I just don't tell them anything,* and so on. So, there's our challenge: it can take a great deal of work as parents to connect with our 7th grade resisters.

I have worked to maintain positive relationships with my children (and now my grandchildren), but I have an advantage: I've worked in my kids' schools. This opportunity has allowed me to teach my children's friends and to be "in the know" about happenings in their world. Obviously, the most parents don't work in their children's schools. But they can stay connected in other ways. Here's what I suggest:

Get involved

Schools are constantly begging for volunteer help. Parents can serve on committees, sell snacks during athletic events, and even substitute teach if time allows. I always say this isn't an opportunity to be "in their business"; it's an opportunity to be "*beside* their business." In other words, you're close enough to see what they're doing to the point that you can start conversations with them about their interests, but they won't see you as a meddling parent.

Create a Home Base

Be the house where all the friends hang out. I always felt more comfortable when my children were home. But they wanted to be with their friends. So I suggested the friends come to us. Maybe it was the middle school teacher in me, but I always planned activities and snacks that kept my children happy and home! That gave me a birds-eye view of every kid's behavior, not just my own.

Avoid Embarrassment

Even though children have embarrassed parents since time eternal, I try really hard not to repay the favor. Just this week my granddaughter wasn't feeling well. I walked into her middle school classroom during class change and discreetly whispered, "Will it embarrass you if I check your forehead for a fever?" She had no problem with it, but if I had just bounced in there and touched her head, she may have felt uncomfortable. Try to keep the embarrassing questions and conversations for your private time together.

Plan Time Together

And speaking of your time together, it's easier to stay connected when you have common interests. I try to stay on top of the latest pop culture, sports teams, and social media trends so that I have something in common with my tweens (or at least I understand what they're talking about). And if it becomes more and more difficult to agree on what you both enjoy, at least support their interests. Rides to gymnastics and basketball practice can provide opportunities for powerful conversations (I used to say I could only talk to my son when he was trapped with me in a car.)

Closing Advice: Hang in There

I periodically tell confused and upset middle school parents that it will get better. The distracted tween eventually gets older and becomes "enlightened." They will thank you for all you've done and perhaps one day strive to be the parent you are!

Recently, while directing traffic in the carpool line, I had a conversation with the middle school principal about the challenges of raising a middle school child. She said her advice is the same as the advice she gives teachers on teaching them: "Treat them like people." Even if they behave like howler monkeys.

Chapter 6
MOTIVATION AND OVERCOMING PROCRASTINATION

Teacher tips and tricks that
might work at home too

Stacey Donaldson, PhD
2010 Mississippi Teacher of the Year

I long ago stopped trying to understand the difference between who my 7th graders thought they were and how they actually acted. The child and would-be young adult are at war with each other in a typical 7th grader. At first glance, the 7th grade student wants to be grown up and treated that way. On the other hand, a simple paper cut unravels the façade as they run to their teacher to bandage the almost invisible wound. Of course, there's a tinge of tongue and cheek in that analysis. Having taught 7th graders for a number of years, I really had to have a sense of humor and love for teaching learners in that age group. It also helps to know a little about how these teens' brains work and understand the value of partnering with family to gain and give support.

Forging a Family-Teacher Partnership

Every 7th grader I have ever taught has been different. They have their strengths and weaknesses, and they bring them to school each day. Regardless of their zip code, all students also have a desire to succeed on that day even if they haven't quite figured out how to. It's the teacher's privilege to sift through the attributes of hundreds of students during those first days of school, and what's observed is not always authentic. Seventh graders, like all learners, are looking to give an impression of themselves that they believe is favorable. They want to fit into the social circle—even if they choose to be square or oval. In my experience, it takes at least one term or grading period to peel back some layers to learn who students are and what they can really do. This hard work starts by laying foundations that forge a safe, respectful community, which is strengthened when family connection is incorporated.

Making strong connections with students' families is essential, as parents can help fill gaps about particular kids. That includes what makes their children happy, sad, angry, or excited. At the same time, there are things teachers will be able to inform parents about their ever-evolving student in this whole new world of middle school.

When students enter middle school, parents sometimes question who switched out their child. The kid who was once open is now a little more reserved; the kid who once laughed and joked with the family at dinner now finds greater pleasure in their mobile device; the kid who once seemed underfoot is now invisible and hanging out in their room more often. This is quite common, as students are really trying to find themselves in this new situation that probably involved moving to a different campus, with new teachers and greater expectations, and older friends, especially if the middle and high schools are joined. Administrators work to create an environment that creates an age group divide, but like any living organism, when there's a will there's a way, and students find a way to connect. That may be through extracurricular activities like band, sports, choir, etc.

Change and growth are happening to your 7th grader right now! This is normal and exciting. Yet adjustments have to be made by teens and their parents to ensure the students have a healthy transition that prepares them to continue to excel.

Procrastination: What Is It?

Procrastination is a long and misunderstood word that has touched many of us at some point, if we are honest. It's one reason I chose to write this chapter. While working on my doctoral degree, I picked up this bad habit. When I procrastinated, I blamed this behavior on exhaustion, even though I would meet all my deadlines. Upon doing some research, I learned and realized that though I may have been tired, that was not why I was procrastinating. I was really afraid I would not be able to do the work perfectly. However, when I started a task (later than I should have, of course) I found I was able to successfully do the task or assignment and complete it on time. I wanted to learn why I was procrastinating and what I could do to stop it. So, here's what I found out.

Procrastination occurs when one postpones a task or delays making a decision. When procrastination occurs in the education process, students fail to fulfill their course responsibilities in a timely manner, which is common among secondary school–aged students. The longer one procrastinates, the more challenging it might be to break the habit.

As mentioned earlier, a number of changes are happening during adolescent years. Not only are students progressing academically, but their personalities are still evolving. During this adolescent period, students might be exposed to risky behaviors, such as internet addiction, alcohol/substance use, bullying, and gang activity, which may negatively impact their biological, psychological, and social development. Parents might hope their children would not be exposed to such behaviors, but children do not have to leave home to gain exposure, thanks to social media.

You may be wondering what causes procrastination during middle school. These days, students are exposed to so much media via television, computers, and cell phones. Top that with social media activity, and we have an issue with time management. Let's revisit the risky behavior of internet addiction. During adolescence, it has a negative impact on a kid's sense of belonging at school (school attachment). Internet addiction also feeds academic procrastination behaviors, which adversely affect academic motivation. As internet usage increases, so does academic procrastination. Internet addiction also takes a toll on psychological and physical development, as well as social relations. Procrastination has also been connected to low motivation, depression, and stress caused by test anxiety and perfectionism. On the other hand, students who have traits of conscientiousness, extroversion, agreeableness, and openness to experience are more likely to have emotional stability that guards against academic procrastination, according to educators Yasin Demir and Mustafa Kutlu.

Motivation's Impact on Procrastination

Educator Kendra Cherry defines motivation as "the process that initiates, guides, and maintains goal-oriented behaviors." Motivation is the reason why students may start their homework in a timely fashion or not delay when making difficult decisions. Motivation is a critical factor in school and academic success. When students like school they are more likely to have a higher level of motivation to do well in school. School attachment is connected to how much students like school and is closely linked to their positive relationships with classmates and teachers. The higher the level of school attachment, the more academically motivated students are. This motivation leads to improved academic performance and decreased likelihood of adopting academic procrastination behaviors, again as Yasin Demir and Mustafa Kutlu report.

Abraham Maslow's hierarchy of needs is a great guide that helps educators learn the importance of school and family connection. Maslow argued humans have a natural desire to be the best they can be, which is called self-actualization, the highest level of the hierarchy of needs pyramid. But before this advanced need is reached, Maslow argued basic needs must be met first. Most of these needs are connected to students' home lives.

The following are the five levels of Maslow's hierarchy:

1. Physical needs, like food and shelter.
2. Safety and security.
3. Friendship and love.
4. Accomplishment and self-esteem.
5. Self-actualization, through self-awareness and personal growth.

When parents and teachers communicate, they can help each other win what may be an apparent battle with their 7th grader. They also form a coalition that their teen will recognize and be more likely to cooperate with.

In her article, "What is Motivation?," Kendra Cherry considers intrinsic and extrinsic factors. Intrinsic motivation develops from *within* the individual and may be connected to something challenging, like playing an instrument or solving a Rubik's Cube in a certain time frame. Parents can use what they know about their 7th grader in helping them consider what motivates them intrinsically. Extrinsic motivations result from *outside* the individual and may be connected to some type of praise, monetary reward, or social recognition.

The following are some ways Kendra Cherry suggests motivation may help parents help their 7th graders:

1. **Motivation improves how one works toward a goal.** Goal orientation is lower when students are not academically motivated. Learning to plan is a skill that many work on over a lifetime. Parents can help their 7th grader by regularly checking in to determine class expectations and completion of assignments, like homework and projects. Depending on the student's course load and extracurricular activities, parents can model how to use a planner and calendar. Asking for suggestions from the teacher can also be helpful.

2. **Motivation encourages one to take action.** Modeling and practicing time management can also be beneficial. Allotting a specific time to begin homework and factoring in breaks for lengthy assignments is a good practice. Usually if a plan is in place and frequent checks are made on progress, students are more likely to act on what they should be doing. Having a plan limits aimlessness that may lead to postponing academic tasks.

3. **Motivation promotes healthy behaviors.** Parents need to be watchful, especially about how their child uses their cell phone, internet, and gaming. Too much of anything is not good. Limiting access to technology at bedtime and restricting use at certain times of the day are boundaries a parent can set for students. This form of restriction will not only improve the quality of rest a student gets, which has psychological, social, and academic benefits, but it will also improve alertness and school performance.

4. **Motivation helps one avoid risky behaviors and addiction.** Research confirms internet addiction and excessive technology

lead to academic procrastination behaviors, which has a negative impact on school attachment and academic motivation. Keeping track of how long your child is using technology could prevent academic procrastination that hinders academic performance.

5. **Motivation improves one's control of life.** A parent's role in helping teens with goal orientation transfers to the student's ability to fulfill academic tasks. When students are motivated academically, they have greater confidence in personal ability. According to Demir and Kutlu, academic self-efficacy skills are not developed when students are not motivated enough academically.

6. **Motivation improves one's happiness and well-being.** When parents meet the basic needs of children, it lays a foundation for the education system to help them in realizing their dreams. When students procrastinate it can cause academic stress, failure, and unhappiness.

Here are some ways to improve motivation, according to Kendra Cherry:

1. Check the goal; if you can, tailor it to meet your interests.

2. If a task is overwhelming, seek ways to make it more achievable by creating smaller steps.

3. Work on confidence.

4. Recall past victories and successful outcomes.

5. Make a list of things that need to be done; mark tasks off as they are completed.

6. Set a timer for 25 minutes, and when it's up, take a four-minute break.

Closing Advice

Motivation is considered an essential factor in the learning process to gain knowledge. Maslow's hierarchy of needs supports the need for parents and teachers to work together, as each holds pieces of the puzzle that mean success for the students. When parents and teachers work together, they are better able to fill learning gaps for their students. Academic procrastination is less likely to wreak havoc when one is academically motivated. Being proactive in setting boundaries for students' use of technology and practicing planning and time management at home support healthy habits that follow students to school.

Remember that 7th grade students are experiencing change and challenges that come with increased expectations that may take them some time to adjust to. Not all students are alike, and what works for one may not work for the other. Take into consideration what you know about your child and look for activities that increase academic motivation, which might help prevent procrastination.

> ### Conversation Starters
>
> - Can you give me an example of something in school that makes you happy, sad, angry, or excited?
> - What friends have you made in other grades through extracurricular activities?
> - What is the definition of procrastination? Have you found yourself putting assignments off?
> - Do you feel anxious about taking tests? Do you feel you need perfect scores?

- How attached do you feel to your teachers and other students in school?
- What kind of schoolwork motivates you to complete it? Would you like to learn some ways to improve your motivation?

Chapter 7
OVERCOMING ACADEMIC SETBACKS

How to turn defeats into learning opportunities and build resiliency

Barbara J. Hopkins, PhD
1988 Nebraska Teacher of the Year

In my classroom I welcome students exactly as they come to me, along with whatever gifts and challenges they may have. I hope you accept that as the premise for all educators and schools. Please count on the teachers and staff to be your partners in your 7th grader's learning.

In this chapter I will share some tips on how to help prevent, or intervene with, academic setbacks and have a great 7th grade year.

Share Knowledge about the Student—Academic Setback Prevention

My first goal each school year is to get to know the students and aid them in getting to know each other. My students come from multiple elementary schools and may not have had classes together before. To help them feel safe in their new learning environment, I make sure they get to know the other students. If a teacher of your 7th grader does not do this, you might encourage your adolescent to get to know a few others in each class. Give them tips to get acquainted. Help them practice introducing themselves to someone who sits beside them in class. Or encourage them to join a club where they will have more opportunity to socially engage with other students. This is important to their sense of belonging and safety, which will aid in their learning and school success.

I also want to know about each student's learning styles and needs. I think it is helpful when a student shares anything they know about how they prefer to learn, or what their setbacks might be. Most kids know if they aren't organized, don't spell well, or have trouble reading. I ask them to share with me, privately, what helps them to learn or how they learn best. This shows I care about them personally, as well as their learning. I like to know what things interest them outside of school (i.e., family, friends, sports, reading, music, gaming). This allows me to build examples into lessons that relate to their interests, which enhances learning. It also shows I care about them, individually. You may help by encouraging your 7th grader to share, as appropriate, with the teacher. Kids learn best from teachers who show an interest and know them individually. You and your adolescent can help with this.

As a reading specialist and English teacher in middle school, I have worked with many students who have had academic setbacks, or even identified learning needs. At this point in their student career, your 7th grader is experienced at school. You already have great knowledge about this topic, as does the student. Trust that knowledge and partner with the school and teacher. I always enjoy it when a student discusses with me anything that would be helpful to them in my classroom (i.e., sitting closer to the front for hearing impairments, getting nervous when they must read aloud to the class). I'm trained and skilled at diagnosis, but always welcome information from the student and parent/guardian so I can be the very best partner in their school success.

If your 7th grader has any identified learning special circumstances (i.e., learning disabled, gifted/talented, hearing impairment, speech impairment, language other than English at home) it is helpful to make sure each teacher is aware, particularly if the student is new to the school or if records have not yet arrived. Please don't leave important information like this up to records being transferred and communicated with the teacher. I always like to hear from the student and/or parent/guardian, so we can establish our collaboration as we start the school year. Knowledge helps avoid academic setbacks.

Pay Attention to Student Needs: It's Science

In anticipating what to do in case of academic or learning setbacks, I'd like to share why student needs matter. It is literally science. Why? Our physical needs, the need to be safe and secure, are basic needs that must be met before we are very functional as productive human beings. If things are not going well at school and there are setbacks, it is important to consider the whole of the student's existence, including assessing their broader needs. The need for love and belonging are necessary to do one's best. For this reason, I encourage you to be attentive to those needs and partner with the teacher if you have any concerns. No one should approach this with judgment. A student's feelings may be their reality, but it doesn't mean that's the way it is. But if a situation is impairing them in any way, then it should be addressed.

Seventh grade can be more challenging in a young person's life than any other time, in my experience. I encourage you to remember to love the child you have in your life and welcome them into being an adolescent, with all that entails. As they experience the changes in their bodies and lives, take the time to remind them of your love and help them to feel secure. It is a time of change, and reassurance is helpful. Many of my former students have shared how hard this time of life was for them. When I asked for input from their experience in my classroom and school, they reiterated that the key was to remember just to love them for who they are and to be a safe space. As their teacher, I always try to give them a safe, caring, and enjoyable place to learn and grow.

That safe and caring environment is important for home and school. It is consistent with Maslow's hierarchy of needs theory (1943). This tried-and-true methodology (see page 61) is still very relevant today. These basics are important for all of us. If academic setbacks occur repeatedly, we should be asking if the needs of the student are being met, beginning with the basic needs of nutrition, rest, and safety. Since many of us in the U.S. do not rest enough or eat as nutritiously as we should, these needs may need to be examined. Being anxious about school, school assignments, or interactions with other students are also very important needs for a 7th grader and should be addressed in our conversations with them.

The need for friends and belonging is essential to an adolescent's sense of well-being, which allows them to focus on learning. Clubs and sports offer opportunities to meet other students so they can find their place in their school life. A happy student is a happier learner. Notice if your adolescent is talking about friends and eating lunch with others. Be aware of the importance of socialization in school and the impact it can have on academic success.

Try to ask questions beyond "how was your day?" It's too easy to answer "fine" or only respond with a grunt. Watch to see if your 7th grader is excited about going to school or shows anxiety. Making sure they are safe, in a caring environment at home and school, and have a sense of belonging and self-esteem are essential.

If these needs are not being met, discuss it with your 7th grader. Also consider visiting with a school counselor or teacher if it continues to be an issue.

Here is my own checklist as a parent and teacher:

Need	Questions to ask (or things to notice)
Physiological	Are you tired? Hungry? What did you have at lunch today at school? How are the lunches? (Note if sleeping or eating patterns have changed.)
Safety	Do you feel safe at school? Do you have enough time to get to each class during passing time? Do you feel safe at home? Is anything making you feel unsafe? Is anyone bullying you? (Note if adolescent seems irritable or reports health issues.)
Belonging	Do you have friends to eat lunch with at school? Are there clubs or activities you want to be a part of? (Note if adolescent is not engaging with others via phone or in person. Drop them off at school or pick them up to see if they seem to have friends. Drive your adolescent and others to an event and listen to their conversations.)
Self esteem	(Note any academic or emotional stress signs. See if habits have changed. Watch if posture or sleeping patterns change.)

Help with Basic Needs

There are times in life when basic needs are difficult to meet for families and this can impact academic success. Some students may have an ill parent or loved one or be new to the area. Please let a teacher or counselor know if the family is homeless, utilities are shut off, or you don't have food. Let the school know if there is a safety issue. There are counselors or social workers who will be able to help access the proper social services. These items all impact academics but are not always known or noticed by teachers until students suffer the academic setbacks. Educators are not there to judge you. They are there to help. Contact them immediately with a basic need to aid in preventing academic setbacks. Communication is helpful. Know that we care.

Reflection Methodology for Problem-Solving

Academic setbacks happen to us all at some point, be it one quiz or test, or an entire course. Missing an assignment or not understanding it is more of a one-time event, hopefully. For one-time events, as opposed to larger issues, I recommend the following methodology:

Reflection Methodology			
Elements			Question
What?	Objective	Facts	What happened to cause this academic setback (i.e., low grade, missing paper)?
Gut?	Reflective	Emotional	How do you feel about this? Why? (multiple responses possible)
So What?	Intuitive	Thought	What does this mean to you now or in the future (i.e., a low grade, anxiety, embarrassment, failure)?
Now What?	Decisional	Action	What do you want to do about it (i.e., retake the quiz, do better next time by studying more, ask teacher for help, get more sleep, remember to bring book home to study)?

I learned this from a United Nations Institute of Cultural Affairs training and it is what I typically use to problem-solve with students. It continues to serve me, and I hope it helps you as well.

In processing, many of us jump immediately into fixing a problem. We tend to leap right past the facts, emotions, and thinking—into action. The key questions in this methodology—what, gut, so what, and now what?—engage multiple senses and allows us to take our body through the steps. This method also allows time to process, rather than to get defensive or disheartened.

If these questions do not get to "why" there is an academic setback, probe further. For all the questions in this process, your role is to *listen*. Ask questions and listen. "Wait time" is an important tool for both the teacher and the parent/guardian in this situation. Kids will wait and hope you give them the answer or fix it for them, as we did when they were younger. Be patient and let them process.

By beginning with facts, you take the emotion out of the academic setback for you and the student. No drama! That is the goal, at least. Then ask questions about the emotions, along with why they feel the way they do. This moves them into that realm after the explanation of facts, and hopefully, it will be more analytical than emotional. Adding the meaning draws out the ramifications of the academic setback. Does this one grade or late paper impact the entire course or is it just embarrassing? What does it mean as far as learning and grades? This identifies the problem in a different perspective with a broader view. Also, hopefully, it makes a problem that seems overwhelming more manageable. Then, you move into having the student take ownership for what they might try to do about this issue in the next steps, with "now what?"

This reflection process has been very successful for students and adults alike when working through an issue. Students usually know if a late/missing assignment, grade on a quiz/test, or other academic issue can be made up, or how it will be addressed by the teacher. If it is not, that should be part of the inquiry the students make for themselves. Was this instance a first time or rare issue? If there is some external factor impacting academic performance, the student should make sure to share that as well. If life situations (like a death in the family, changing family situation, being bullied, feeling overwhelmed with school, etc.) are interfering with learning, share those with the teacher.

A Student Empowered

Teachers are used to discussions around the "why" and, hopefully, give options to resolve any impact on the desired grade or course. The student should take the lead on reaching out to the teacher to resolve this issue, even if it is to say, "I just don't get it." This is an important time in life to make sure the student takes responsibility for their learning, with your loving support. Be the coach, not the director or problem-solver. This sets them up for long-term success.

One-time or rare academic setbacks are easier to resolve than longer term patterns. If there are recurring issues, you should set a time to speak with the teacher(s), with your 7th grader included, and determine if there is a more coordinated approach that is needed. Encouraging your 7th grader to take responsibility for their role as a learner is important, but they still may need you for bigger issues. There are many academic supports that exist to help your 7th grader with their studies, and their teachers and counselor can help you find them. Count on them to help!

Parent-Teacher-Student

I encourage students to attend parent/guardian teacher conferences if they can. There should not be any surprises to the student, and it lays the responsibility for their learning on them. Parents, guardians, and teachers are there to support that role. Attending these conferences allows the student to aid in addressing any academic setbacks directly, instead of discussing it via the adults. When my students have academic celebrations or challenges (academic or behavioral) we always try to contact the parent/guardian together. This saves the back and forth that may happen when everyone is not in on the conversation. Likewise, if you wish to call a teacher, include your adolescent in the conversation.

If the adults in a student's life do not speak English, or need assistance due to hearing loss, ask for a trained interpreter from the school. Do not leave that role to the student, since their role is to be the learner. The school has a responsibility to provide an interpreter.

Support

Assuming all is well in the eating, safety, and sleeping arena, delving into the feeling of belonging is key to a 7th grader's well-being. What does this have to do with academic setbacks? Emotions and hormones are different when kids reach this age, so be supportive, even when you are asking yourself, "what is the big deal?" As noted in the hierarchy of needs, these basics can very much get in the way.

If you can help your 7th grader identify the cause of an issue, you are more likely to be able to support them in problem-solving. Be encouraging, but let them know that you are there to help them brainstorm, and you believe in them to solve the problem.

Multiple teachers

Because your adolescent is now dealing with multiple teachers and needs to organize differently, it is helpful to assess if academic setbacks are in one class or multiple classes. Support exists for learning issues, health needs, or other situations that can impact learning. Allow the school to partner with you on interventions for long-term needs. Begin with one teacher for help. Ask for additional assistance through a counselor or the administration if you need more help.

Closing Advice

Trust yourself as the loved one of your 7th grader. Know that safety and love are essential as you work to provide for their needs. Sharing any learning needs or special situations with a teacher can help prevent academic setbacks. Should they arrive, also consider the needs your adolescent has that may impair their learning. If there are no outside influences, use the reflection methodology to aid your 7th grader in addressing the academic setback. And remember that the school has services either to help or to contact to aid you with other needs that impair your student's ability to learn. Most of all, enjoy life with your 7th grader; it's a fun time!

Conversation Starters

- What interests you outside of the classroom or school? Do you feel you can share these interests with your teacher(s)?
- Do you feel safe at school? Is anyone bullying you?
- Do you have enough time to get to each class?
- What would make you feel unsafe?
- What do you feel the problem is? What do you think caused your problem at school?
- How do you feel about it, and why do you think you feel this way?
- How will the setback affect you in the future?
- What can you do to improve the situation?
- What can I do to help you prepare to handle this?

Chapter 8
DIFFERENT LEARNING STYLES AND ACCOMMODATIONS

How to support your child who is struggling in the classroom

Tyler Bartlett
2015 Wyoming Teacher of the Year

Nikki Bartlett
7th grade ELA teacher

"Making the decision to have a child is momentous. It is to decide forever to have your heart go walking around outside your body," as education journalist Elizabeth Stone said. Parenting is not for the faint of heart. No pun intended. It is difficult to watch your child struggle, especially when they're working hard and yet still on the verge of giving up. For this and many reasons, 7th grade is a difficult age. Academic rigor is increasing and new social opportunities are emerging, all while the body is being flooded with emotions (and hormones). It's a particularly trying year for your child and you. As you journey through this tough year with your heart outside your body, your child is likely to encounter difficult challenges. The best way to help might be summarized in five "E's": **Embrace** the struggle,

empathize with your child, **empower** them to take on the challenge, **evaluate** the situation, and **enter** if (and how) you are needed.

Embrace the Struggle

The most important thing to keep in mind while you observe your child struggling, experiencing discomfort, and even pain, is that facing challenges is actually key to their future success. In his book, *The Obstacle Is the Way*, author and stoicism advocate Ryan Holiday brilliantly makes clear that nobody can stop, or even predict, when difficulties will arise. All we can control is how we respond. Each trial we face can teach us a valuable lesson that better prepares us for the next inevitable obstacle we will face. This means we focus on preparing the child for the path, not the path for the child.

Life is a struggle, and this is the time for your child to experience it—while they are still safely surrounded by your support and love. Too often, parents hinder their students from joining too many activities, as that may pose the potential for stress and setbacks. Or parents, observing their child struggling with a science project, for example, step in and do much of the work for them. These actions may be well-intentioned and come from a place of love, but it robs the child of the opportunity to learn and grow. Getting kids more busy and more involved in a variety of activities offers opportunities to learn better time management. A reasonable level of difficulty with homework is necessary to learning. Allowing your child to struggle will create a more successful student in the classroom, a more well-rounded young person, and a more resilient adult. If this sounds too harsh, take a deep breath; it's important for your child to experience struggles, but they won't have to do so alone.

Empathize with Your child

One of us (Nikki), a 7th grade English teacher, teaches a lesson on empathy, sympathy, and apathy every year. The lesson includes a note that the prefix *em-* means *put in or into* and *-path* is a suffix derived from the Greek *pathos* meaning *suffering or disease*, making *empathy* literally *putting yourself into someone's suffering*. We all feel sympathy more naturally than we do empathy; sympathy involves understanding someone's pain or suffering while empathy involves putting yourself in another's shoes and understanding *why* they may be having these feelings. Empathy is a trait that no one is born with but we can learn by being shown. This challenging year gives you a great opportunity to model empathy to your child so they can learn how to treat others empathetically as well.

As a parent of a 7th grader (or a prepubescent teen), you know they are not the greatest empath in your life. If anything, they fit the definition of *apathetic* better because it's easier to not feel; it's easier to not acknowledge different emotions. To get them through their struggle, whether it be big or small, academic or otherwise, parents and teachers must be the village that surrounds them with love and empathy. Parents and teachers have survived the middle school years, and we need to share that empathy with our struggling students.

The best way to do this is to validate their feelings. As much as you may want to, don't jump in to fix whatever they're struggling with. Most times at this age, they're not looking for a fix. They're looking for love. When your 7th grader is faced with a struggle, spend more time listening than talking. Be a safe place for them to talk about and work through their feelings.

While it's important to communicate to them that you, too, have been through something similar, try to steer clear of telling too many stories of your own middle school struggles. Everyone's struggles are different, and we don't want to overshadow their struggle with our own. Your path and their path aren't the same; the way in which your struggle was worked through may not be feasible for them now. We can't edit their path or their solution, but we can prepare them by hearing them, loving them, and acknowledging their feelings. Never underestimate the value of truly listening to your child vent their frustrations, interjecting the occasional "that stinks" or "I'm so sorry that happened." What a great way to model empathy while being there for your child.

Empower Them to Take on the Challenge

It sounds well and good to say that we should embrace struggles and just listen when our kids need us, but eventually problems need to be solved. The key here is parents can't be expected to be the fixer. You're the guide on their journey but your goal is to equip them to take on the challenge themselves.

At the start of every year at Newcastle Middle School, one of us (Tyler) gives essentially the same speech to students and parents. The first part of the message is simply that twelve- and thirteen-year-old children are expected to make mistakes and experience difficulties. We look forward to these mistakes as an opportunity to learn how to take ownership and do something about it. Which leads to the second part of the discussion, taken from organizational coach and Focus 3 founder Tim Kight: E + R = O, or Event + Response = Outcome. Rather than getting derailed by the event (i.e., struggling with a difficult class, falling behind due to absences, feeling crunched for time with lots of activities going on), students should focus on their best response in order for the best possible outcome. We don't have control over the events that happen to us, but we do control how we respond.

To help you feel a little more in control, try talking to your child about some time management strategies. Does their school offer an after-school homework center? Do they need a planner to stay organized and make sure deadlines are being met? Would a "do now, do later" task list help them feel more in charge? Think of how you, an adjusted adult, tackle all the tasks you have going on in your everyday life. Chunking up the day or tasks can help alleviate some of the stress you and your child may be feeling when overwhelmed by all the activities going on around them.

So, what does that mean for you? Tell your child to take a deep breath and a step back. Assess the situation and the possible root causes. Have they reached out to a teacher or coach? Have they visited with the school counselor? Are they taking full advantage of all the resources available at their school? As much as possible, resist answering these questions for your child. Middle school is a key step in the transition from childhood to adulthood, which means gaining some well-earned independence even with a safety net of caring adults at home. Do you really want to be calling your child's boss in 15 years to help them resolve a workplace conflict? Avoiding situations like that start by empowering them now. And remember, they're not doing this alone. You've empathized with them, and now you're giving them tips and tools necessary to work through this...on their own.

Evaluate the Situation

You've embraced the struggle, you've listened to them vent without rushing to solve the problem, and when they were ready, you gave them the help they needed to try to take on the challenge independently. Now what?

We wait. We live in an instant gratification world in so many ways, but there are still things that take time to come to fruition. If your child is working on getting their pre-algebra grade up, don't expect a D to become an A overnight. If they're overwhelmed with school, student council, and soccer all happening at once, the time management strategies they came up with will take time to take effect.

Your goal at this point is to give it time and check in with your child. Just because they aren't crying every night doesn't mean they don't still need you to check on them and see how things are progressing. Whether it's at dinner, during the car ride home, or while you're doing the dishes together, ask them for a progress report. Keep informed about how they're feeling. Eventually, if all goes well, the struggle will be a thing of the past and something you can both look back on with pride in how your both managed it. However, we know not every problem is solved so easily, which leads us to the last step of our process.

Enter the Situation if (and how) You Are Needed

Rest assured: we understand that sometimes parents just need to get more directly involved. Our previous recommendations are based on years in education, where we sometimes have encountered the occasional overaggressive parent. You've likely heard of helicopter parents, bulldozer dads, and tiger moms. All of these parents are well-intentioned and doing what they think is best for their child. However, the labels carry negative connotations because it implies that the parent stepped in *before* giving their child the chance to tackle the situation on their own.

But if you have followed the rest of the advice in this chapter, you haven't jumped the gun. You embraced the struggle, you empathized with your child and empowered them to tackle the problem independently. Now, after evaluating the situation and visiting with them, you realize there is still work to be done. It's time to get involved.

Maybe we're just lucky to work in the school district we do, but the educators we know and work with every day want what is best for children. They honestly care. So, when it's time to contact the teacher, coach, or administrator, remember that you're on the same team. Reach out politely and let them know you have an issue that you'd like to follow up on. Of course, you want to voice your concerns and advocate for your child, but also be sure to ask questions and listen. See what perspective the school might have and what solutions or interventions they might have already offered or tried. Be open to their suggestions while honestly and clearly advocating for your child. If you take a partnership approach with the school, your child is more likely to receive the help they need without any hard feelings along the way.

One final note on parenting styles: when parents try to remedy the situation before allowing their students to struggle, they can unintentionally become a "bulldozer" or a "helicopter" parent. During that struggle, become a coach instead. Coaches want what is best for their players. They want individual success as well as achievement for the team as a whole. This means coaches can't have tunnel vision for one individual player or situation; they have to keep the big picture in mind while planning for current *and* future success. They hold their athletes accountable and intentionally create difficult situations to use as teachable moments that promote improvement and growth. Coaches guide their players on what to do, but the players are the ones that must perform. And, of course, coaches encourage their athletes through good times and bad. A great coach sounds like a pretty good role model for the parent of a 7th grader.

Closing Advice

At Newcastle Middle School, we talk a lot about teaching using the "gradual release of responsibility" model. It can be simplified down to three basic steps for providing instruction on new concepts or skills:

1. I do.
2. We do.
3. You do.

The idea is that we must start by demonstrating and modeling new concepts first. We show students what to do and how to do it. Then, we practice together. The students take on more roles and more ownership, but teachers are still participating side-by-side with students. Lastly, when they are ready, we let students take on the task independently. This isn't to say that they've mastered the concept (far from it, actually). This is just the next step in the learning process. We'll never really know what they learned unless we let them try (and sometimes fail) on their own.

So it goes with being the parent of a 7th grader. You've spent their life serving as a role model and working closely with them. Now is the time for some independent practice. This doesn't mean they've mastered all there is to learn, and it doesn't mean that they won't still need help and guidance along the way. But by following the five E's we've laid out here, we believe you can effectively "coach" your 7th grader through the next set of challenges on life's journey. Best of luck to you and your child!

> ### Conversation Starters
>
> - What is the difference between empathy and sympathy?
> - Is there anything in school you are struggling with?
> - Can you take a step back and assess the situation? What are your thoughts about why you are struggling?
> - What might be the best response? Have you reached out to your teacher, coach, or counselor?
> - What other resources might help you?
> - How has the situation progressed?
> - Under what circumstances would you need me to step in and reach out to your teacher/coach/counselor?

Chapter 9
CHALLENGING STUDENT-TEACHER RELATIONSHIPS

How to support your child if they aren't meshing with their teacher

Jamey Olney
2000 DoDEA Teacher of the Year

My daughter burst into my classroom after school the first week of 7th grade. She exclaimed, "I don't like my English teacher. He is so boring. I want to change classes." When I asked her why, she replied, "All he teaches is grammar and how to diagram sentences."

I am a 7th grade English teacher myself. I took a pause and restrained myself from commenting, as my daughter mumbled and grumbled through her homework. I simply said, "If you're frustrated with an assignment, ask your teacher for help."

Fast forward two years. My daughter, who was once a reluctant reader, is taking advanced placement English in high school. English is one of her favorite subjects and she credits this teacher with becoming a strong writer. Because of the skills she learned in his class, she has gone on to write award-winning speeches, memoirs, and scholarship essays. If I had given into her first request to "change classes," she may have been in a very different place. Through this experience, my daughter learned valuable lessons in not making snap judgments, working with different personalities, and persisting through difficulty.

Seventh grade is a transitional year for students. They have left the security of one or two teachers the past seven years of elementary school to navigate an often bewildering maze of six to seven teachers daily with different deadlines, class expectations, and teaching styles. Add to this mix the complexity of relating to six different sets of peers, extracurricular activities, and a hefty dose of tween/teen hormones, and you have a recipe for at least one class and teacher your student may not click with. Seventh grade students have the heavy lift of learning how to manage their time while juggling both the content and expectations of several teachers.

School-Home Communication

It's important to make the first interaction with your student's teachers a positive one. Attend back-to-school night, learn how to navigate the student grading platform, reach out to your student's teachers via email or the school's parent communication system. This will go a long way in establishing rapport and keeping the lines of communication open. Ask about opportunities for additional support before and after school in the event your student needs it. Being proactive in establishing relationships can prevent or diminish misunderstandings. Remember that when your student brings you concerns, you are only hearing one side of the issue.

As students are making the shift to more independence, they are learning the valuable skill of advocating for themselves and knowing how and when to seek help and solve problems. However, 7th graders often don't have the language to articulate what they are feeling or needing. With caseloads of up to 200 students, teachers don't always have the time to follow up with each student. More responsibility to seek help or clear up misunderstandings falls on the shoulders of students.

Characteristics of 7th Grade Students

Tween moods are changeable and unpredictable as their bodies and personalities are rapidly changing. It's an age of dramatic contrasts. They want adults to notice, listen, and talk to them but also to leave them alone. They're engaged one minute and bored the next. Outgoing with friends and moody and withdrawn at home, their feelings are easily hurt and they can easily hurt others' feelings. Likes and dislikes are more pronounced. For instance, they may "love" science but "hate" English. They may worry and complain about schoolwork. They often have strong opinions about their teachers, both positive and negative, and freely share these opinions with peers and parents.

Your role as a parent is to listen to their concerns, bearing in mind that their judgments are extremely changeable and might not require adult intervention. (Though sometimes it may become clear that your student needs your help to navigate a particular class or teacher. For instance, if the teacher is verbally or physically abusive.) Sometimes students will vent but don't want to talk to the teacher. If your student doesn't want to take the time to discuss the issue with the teacher, it may not be a big deal.

Students who complain that teachers are boring or unfair often mean that teachers are either not giving them enough attention or holding them to high expectations that may be stretching them beyond their comfort zone. Seventh grade students need adults in their lives, both parents and teachers, who will observe closely, listen carefully, and encourage risk-taking.

How Can I Support?

Your student gripes about a teacher or class. This can be a golden opportunity to practice resilience, grit, problem-solving, and conflict resolution. Much has been written about the "helicopter parent." Unfortunately, the "helicopter parent" who hovers over the child has evolved into the "lawnmower" parent who "mows" down any obstacles or conflicts in a child's way, sometimes well into young adulthood. But we must guard against interfering and micromanaging in order to safeguard our children from failure, disappointments, and the slightest hint of struggle. Jumping to the rescue too quickly sends the message to your student that they can't do things for themselves. As a consequence, students can become poorly equipped to handle routine growing experiences, one of these the ability to communicate with teachers and superiors.

Below are three different approaches to dealing with student-teacher conflict.

Student-Driven Approach

Scenario: Your student comes home complaining that their history teacher Ms. Jones never calls on her or answers her questions.

First, determine the root cause of the problem and let your student advocate for herself with guidance. Start with open-ended questions such as:

- When are you trying to ask a question or make a comment?
- What could you have done differently?
- Where can you go for help?
- If you were trying to help a friend in a similar situation, is there anything you might suggest that they could do?

Helping students problem-solve and reflect is a life skill that will benefit them throughout school and beyond. When students practice working through challenges in the sheltered environment of school, they gain valuable coping skills to deal with life's conflicts in less safe environments with fewer supports.

When faced with a conflict, human tendency is to focus on what the other person did or didn't do. This creates a sense of helplessness instead of empowerment. But instead of jumping in to save the day by emailing the teacher for clarification, guide your student into switching the narrative to what they can do. For instance, *"When I have a question during the lesson, I'll write it down. I'll ask the teacher when she isn't in the middle of a lesson or email her after class."* Teachers are imperfect humans along with everyone else. By giving your student the tools to advocate for herself, you're sending the message that it's far easier to focus on what's within one's control than to try and "fix" someone else.

Parent- and Student-Driven Approach

Scenario: Your student is failing math and wants to switch teachers. They say the teacher doesn't explain concepts clearly and just gives students assignments to complete on their own.

The long-term goal here is for your student to learn to be flexible, to be able to adjust to different teaching styles, and to take ownership of their learning. It's important to ask questions rather than jump to conclusions. Offering to immediately talk to the principal about switching teachers would not be the answer here, because it takes the responsibility off your student. In this situation, you might lend a listening ear and brainstorm possible solutions with your student. By asking yourself "Whose problem is this?" you condition your student to cope with situations that are uncomfortable rather than relying on a parent to step in. Defaulting to the latter can lead to helplessness, anxiety, and depression in your child as they realize they can't problem-solve themselves.

You might set up a time for you and your student to meet with the teacher. Provide your student openers such as, *"It hurts my feelings when...I don't understand...I feel like this isn't fair because..."* so that your student can prepare beforehand. At the end of this chapter is a resource with more language for your student to use to articulate concerns. Your role in this instance is coach, mentor, and moral support. Let your student do the talking and facilitate as needed.

Parent-Driven Approach

Scenario: Over a period of several weeks, your student mentions that Mr. Green, the science teacher, does nothing but show Disney movies and let students play Fortnite on their phones. When you ask your student about what she is learning in science, she shows you a coloring page.

This may be a symptom of a larger problem. Still, it's always best to go to the teacher first before going up the chain of command, especially because in most cases, the administration will direct you back to the teacher. Make an appointment to meet with the teacher and request a course outline so you can support at home. Check with your student each week to see what assignments are due. Before you decide to escalate the issue beyond the teacher, weigh the potential costs and benefits. Ask another parent to give their opinion on what's going on. Document emails, phone calls, and meeting notes so you will have a record in the event you need to speak with the counselor or principal.

Closing Advice

Think of 7th grade as a dress rehearsal for life. Working through difficult situations and with difficult people builds confidence. Allowing students to be creative, to problem-solve, and to develop coping skills will help them when they get to college and their roommate has a different definition of "cleanliness"; with a friend who's not being so "friendly" anymore; and with that demanding boss at their first job. When we give students the tools to sit with discomfort, think about options, talk about a situation with someone, and make decisions, we equip them for future success in academics, the workplace, and relationships.

Student Resource: Advocating for Your Education		
Problem	Solutions to Try	Example

(continued)

Student Resource: Advocating for Your Education (cont.)

Problem	Solutions to Try	Example
No Wi-Fi or limited internet access due to technical issues (DO NOT consider yourself excused from the work)	If attempts to get Wi-Fi working (restart computer, router, etc.) are not working, contact tech support As soon as it is up and running again, email your teacher	Dear [Teacher], I wanted to let you know I did not have Wi-Fi for (time period) and so was unable to complete work during that time. I plan to make up the work (during specific time). I will reach out to you when the work is complete/if I have questions. Thank you for understanding. Sincerely, [Name]

(continued)

Student Resource: Advocating for Your Education (cont.)

Problem	Solutions to Try	Example
No Wi-Fi or limited internet access due to switching households (DO NOT consider yourself excused from the work)	Email your teacher	Dear [Teacher], I wanted to let you know I do not/will not have Wi-Fi during [time period] [optional: because I am with X parent/some other reason]. I want to be sure I am keeping up with school during that time so I was thinking I could [download assignments early to work on them offline/make them up once I have access to Wi-Fi again/some other solution]. Is this OK or did you have another idea that you'd prefer I do? Thank you for being flexible. Sincerely, [Name]

(continued)

Student Resource: Advocating for Your Education (cont.)

Problem	Solutions to Try	Example
Not sure why grade is so low (DO NOT give up!)	Check your grade to see what is missing or bringing the grade down + Email your teacher to problem-solve	Dear [Teacher], I noticed I have a [grade] in the portal and when I checked, it appears that I [am missing X assignment/did poorly on Y assessment]. I would like to work hard to bring my grade up. I plan to [make up missing X assignment/retake Y quiz] [on specific date/time]. Would that be acceptable? Is there anything in particular I need to know about making it up/doing a retake? Thank you for being flexible. Sincerely, [Name]

(continued)

Student Resource: Advocating for Your Education (cont.)

Problem	Solutions to Try	Example
Not sure why late work has not been entered in the gradebook yet (DO NOT assume your teacher is "mad at you"; they aren't and they probably just don't realize the work is done) (DO NOT give up!)	Email your teacher to let them know the work is complete and ready to be graded	Dear [Teacher], I have completed [xyz assignment]. I wanted to let you know it is done and ready to be graded. I handed it in to [Schoology/EdPuzzle/etc.]. Please let me know if you have trouble [finding it/opening the file/etc.] Thank you for being flexible. Please let me know if you have any questions. Sincerely, [Name]

(continued)

Student Resource: Advocating for Your Education (cont.)

Problem	Solutions to Try	Example
Not sure about a missing assignment (DO NOT consider yourself excused from the work) (DO NOT give up!)	Email your teacher to get the help you seek OR If your teacher has regular office hours/ videoconferences, attend one or more to get the help you seek	Dear [Teacher], I noticed in the gradebook that I'm missing [assignment]. I'm not sure what this assignment is. Can you please explain it and/or direct me where to find it and what I need to do? I appreciate your help and will get this work completed right away, once I have the information I need to get it done. Thank you for helping me. Sincerely, [Name]

(continued)

Student Resource: Advocating for Your Education (cont.)

Problem	Solutions to Try	Example
Can't find materials or unsure how to complete assignment (DO NOT consider yourself excused from the work) (DO NOT give up!)	Email your teacher to get the help you seek OR If your teacher has regular office hours/ videoconferences, attend one or more to get the help you seek	Dear [Teacher], I was trying to do [specific assignment/classwork for -specific date-] and I am unsure [where to find xyz/what I need to do]. Can you please help? I appreciate it, thank you. Sincerely, [Name]
Struggling to understand course content (DO NOT consider yourself excused from the work) (DO NOT give up!)	Email your teacher to get the help you seek OR If your teacher has regular office hours/ videoconferences, attend one or more to get the help you seek	Dear [Teacher], I am struggling to understand [specific content]. For example, [give a specific question you have; if you just say "it's hard," your teacher does not know how to help you]. Can you please help? If it's something that can't be explained over email, would you be willing to do a videoconference? I appreciate it, thank you. Sincerely, [Name]

(continued)

Student Resource: Advocating for Your Education (cont.)

Problem	Solutions to Try	Example
Feeling overwhelmed by late work (DO NOT consider yourself excused from the work) (DO NOT give up!)	Email your teacher for guidance on how to prioritize then Follow through with the plan that you and your teacher come up with	Dear [Teacher], I have so many missing assignments I don't know where to start. I really want to succeed this quarter, but it is all so overwhelming. What 1–3 assignments do you recommend I tackle first? I will get started on it today, and I will email you if I have additional questions. Thank you for your help, I appreciate it. Sincerely, [Name]

(continued)

Student Resource: Advocating for Your Education (cont.)

Problem	Solutions to Try	Example
Feeling sad/ isolated/ anxious because everything is changing/ different/ scary/you miss your friends or teachers (DO NOT consider yourself excused from the work) (DO NOT give up!)	Email a teacher you trust, and/or your guidance counselor to get support OR If there is a teacher you trust that has office hours or Zoom, consider attending just to talk/interact (even if you don't have questions about class)	Dear [Teacher], I am having a hard time with this. I am feeling [feelings] because [reasons]. [Can expand on your feelings here if you like]. I am reaching out to you because I could really use your support. Would you please [email me back/schedule a Zoom with me] to talk about this? I appreciate it. Sincerely, [Name]

(continued)

Student Resource: Advocating for Your Education (cont.)

Problem	Solutions to Try	Example
Home circumstances causing academic challenges (More than just "virtual learning is different from what I'm used to and is hard!" Examples include moving, health issue, loss/illness of a family member, job loss, taking care of siblings and other family members, major uncertainty about critical life needs: food, shelter, etc.) (DO NOT give up!)	Email your guidance counselor and/or teacher(s) and/or administration + Respond when they reply	Dear [school personnel], I wanted to let you know that right now I am dealing with [crisis situation] and it is very hard for me/my family. I am struggling to complete work, but it is very difficult in these circumstances. I do want to succeed and am asking for your support. Can you please get in touch with me so we can talk about possible solutions? OR: give possible solution ideas yourself. For example, Would it be possible to [excuse or not count X assignments/ grade only Z assignments/ drop my lowest grade/ etc.]? Sincerely, [Name]

(continued)

Student Resource: Advocating for Your Education (cont.)

Problem	Solutions to Try	Example
Home circumstances causing social/ emotional challenges (see list of sample circumstances above) (DO NOT give up!)	Email your guidance counselor and/or teacher(s) and/or administration—any trusted adult in the building + Respond when they reply	Dear [school personnel], I wanted to let you know that right now I am dealing with [crisis situation] and it is very hard for me/my family. My/Our most critical pressure/need right now is [describe]. What resources are available to help? Sincerely, [Name]

(continued)

Student Resource: Advocating for Your Education (cont.)

Problem	Solutions to Try	Example
Feeling unmotivated because everything is different and you want to just coast on your first quarter grade (DO NOT consider yourself excused from the work) (DO NOT give up!)	Do your work anyway, and/or Take responsibility for your decision and email your teacher to problem-solve	Dear [Teacher], I have been feeling really unmotivated because this is such a wild situation. I don't have any family issues or anything like that holding me back. I'll be honest, I haven't been putting a lot of work in because I am counting on my first quarter grade to carry me through. However, I know this is not the right way to go about this and I know I will learn better, and develop more resilience and maturity, by taking responsibility and completing the work. What 1–3 assignments do you suggest I tackle first to get on the right track/have the most impact on my learning? I will get started on it right away and will let you know if I am stuck or have questions. Thank you for understanding. Sincerely, [Name]

Chapter 10
CONSTRUCTIVE PARENT-SCHOOL RELATIONSHIPS

How can a parent best work with the school to support their student's achievement?

Angela Wilson
DoDEA 2012 National Finalist

As a parent of four girls, I have experienced firsthand the joys and sorrows of going through middle school and as a middle school teacher for 14 years, I experience these joys and sorrows every day. It is a tough age, full of wavering emotions. School is not always the priority of the students as they struggle to find their place, understand themselves, and maneuver the changes of growing up. I am sure you, as parents, often feel at a loss. From experience on both sides, I can tell you that the key is developing a partnership with your child's teachers and other school personnel. We have all heard the African proverb, *it takes a village to raise a child*. At the expense of sounding too cliché, it does take a village. Do not try to take this on all by yourself or expect the school to work some kind of magic.

As a previous elementary teacher who transitioned to middle school, I have noticed that by the time a child reaches middle school, many parents have taken the hands-off approach. My parent attendance at open house or back to school nights is less than half of what it was at my elementary school. Our school often must beg parents to join the PTSA at the middle school level. There have been years when one did not exist at that level, because there were not enough parents to join. The communication I receive from middle school parents is minimal. If I do hear from a parent, it is usually something like, "How can Bobby get his grade up?" or "Do you offer any extra credit assignments in your class?" Parent and teacher communication seems to drastically disappear at the middle school ages.

I think many parents assume that their child is now old enough to handle things on their own. It might be that students do not want their parents involved, because it could make them look uncool or like a baby. Whatever the reason, parents, teachers, and other school personnel do not seem to have the same connection as they had in the younger grades. This is unfortunate, since middle school is probably the age when this partnership matters the most.

So, how can parents and schools work together to support student achievement? Below are some suggestions based on actions I take as a parent, what is helpful to me as a teacher, and ideas from other middle school parents and teachers.

Continuous Communication

It is easy as a middle school parent to meet the teacher, or reach out to the teacher, just once and think to yourself, *they will contact me if there are any issues.* Yes, the teacher will likely contact you when issues arise, but this approach to communication does not build relationships. It also puts the onus completely on the teacher, instead of sharing the responsibility. Instead, I suggest you send a "Million Words or Less" letter or email to your child's teachers. It can be the same letter or email to each teacher. This is a popular assignment, so maybe it is something you have already seen. Even if this is so, take it seriously, since it is the first step in building a partnership. A "Million Words or Less" letter is basically a letter to the teacher telling them about your child. As a teacher, I learn so much from these letters. Each letter should include general information about the student, like what they like to do for fun, their hobbies, and how the teacher can help them learn. If the child has struggled with something emotional or academic in the past, this information is extremely helpful. This letter/email is your chance to tell the teacher anything you want to about your child, without having to wait for one of the few parent-teacher conferences scheduled. It does not have to as long as the title of the assignment suggests. I would just make sure it includes information that you think the teachers need to know, so they can best support your child.

My students always think it's fun, because I say, "Your first homework assignment is not for you, but for your parents." This gets them excited to give the assignment to their parents. I know that this may seem annoying or like a lot of extra time you need to spend. I remember getting this assignment as a parent and thinking, *not this again*. However, I quickly changed my tune. I know how valuable this information is and how it helps guide teachers. Is not your child and their achievement in middle school worth your time?

So, if this assignment is not given, give it to yourself. At the beginning of each year, send an email or write a letter, telling the teacher(s) about your child. Remember that the nonacademic stuff is just as important as the academic details. Teachers believe in building relationships. One of the best ways to do that is to share your child's love of soccer with them when the school year starts. Of course, focus on academics too. If you know that your child does not like to be called on in class to read, please note that. You know your child better than anyone. You will give your child a leg up if you can share some strategies and tips that work to motivate or help your child learn. It will take the guessing game out of the learning process and the teacher will not have to start from square one. Below is an example of what your first email or your "Million Words or Less" letter might look like:

Dear Ms. Wilson,

I am writing to introduce my child, Bobby Jones, in a million words or less. Bobby has always been a fun-loving kid. He is a great example to his younger brothers and sister. They look to him for guidance. You can count on Bobby to usually make the right choice, which is something we emphasize a lot at home.

If you talk basketball with Bobby, you will become his new favorite person. He lives and breathes basketball. He plays on an outside league, which requires him to practice from 6–8 p.m. Mondays and Wednesdays. He is often tired the following days. You might notice that. Although his bedtime is 9 p.m., on basketball nights, we are pretty sure he stays up later to finish homework. We have caught him on social media a few times, instead of working. That is something we will deal with. However, if you notice him not being as alert or attentive, please let us know.

We have noticed that Bobby is more reserved since starting middle school. Last year in 6th grade his teachers often said that they wished he would participate more in class. He does enjoy working with a partner or in small groups. We think that gives him a little more courage to speak up, if he has a partner or team supporting him.

His closest friend is Paul Smith. They usually work well together, but they can sometimes get off task. If Paul is in his class, he might be a good support for Bobby. However, we will support your decision to separate them, if they are not focused.

Finally, we feel that it is important that you know that Bobby has struggled with reading since first grade. He has been in various support classes to strengthen his reading skills. He has made improvements. He is very self-conscious about this. Last year, his language arts teacher would call on different students to read, without any notice. This gave Bobby anxiety. He even missed a day of school over it. If you would like Bobby to read aloud, would you please let him know the part ahead of time, so he can practice it? Also, if you have suggestions for us to help him at home with his reading, please let us know.

Thank you for caring enough to ask about our child. We are excited for this 7th grade year. Please know we are here to support you. Thank you for what you do for all students each day. We plan to be proactive in Bobby's education. We look forward to hearing from you and working with you.

Sincerely,
Mr. and Mrs. Jones
Email: jones@gmail.com
Phone: 123-456-7890

Once you have sent your first email/letter, continue to check in. The emphasis on continuous communication is *continuous*. Obviously, write or call when there is a concern, but also be the parent that reaches out when there is not. I would make a goal to write or call a few times a quarter. You do not want the only time you have reached out to the teacher(s) to be the email/letter at the beginning of the year. The continuous communication email can be short and simple. It may look like this:

Dear Ms. Wilson,

I hope things are going well. I am just writing to ask for a quick check-in on Bobby. Is he participating more? Do you have any further suggestions to help Bobby? Thank you for feedback on his last writing assignment. Also, is there anything I can help you with? Thanks again for all you do.

Sincerely,
Mrs. Jones

Be Involved

You want to be the parent that is as involved as possible. I know that all family circumstances are different. Sometimes it is not feasible to be as involved as you would like. However, do as much as you can. When you cannot participate, communicate with the teacher. Explain why you can or cannot be there. Being involved shows the teachers/school personnel that you care. More importantly, it shows your child that you care. So, how can you be involved?

- Attend events sponsored by the school. Go to open house, back to school night, parent teacher conferences, math nights, culture nights, reading nights, school action club luncheons, PTSA meetings, etc. Being a presence at school events says a lot.

- Offer to help teachers. It does not have to be extremely time-consuming to be helpful. For example, this year a parent messaged me and said, "I want to help. I don't have a lot of time, but if you ever need anything cut out or glued, please send it home with my child."

- Ask to be a "_____ Mom, Dad, or Guardian." Ask to be a Band Mom or Math Dad. Even if these roles do not exist, you can suggest them to the teacher. You could write something like, "Hello Ms. Wilson, I would love to be the ELA Mom for period 6. Basically, I am willing to help in any way. Please let me know if this is something that would be helpful to you and how you'd best like to utilize me."

- Pick a project to help with. Once again, the project does not have to be huge. One thing I found super helpful was asking a parent to find new books for my literature circles. The parent went online and researched popular, yet appropriate, middle school books. She compiled the books in a shopping cart for me and I submitted the request for funds. So, pick a project that you are passionate about and would love to see in your child's school or ask the teacher for ideas. Then, take the load off the teacher and run with it.

- Join the parent groups offered. The obvious one is PTSA, but there are also others. Our school used to offer "Parent University." Once a month, different topics about middle school students were offered during a lunch meeting. Parents came to the school and attended the classes they were interested in. This is a great way to build relationships between school and parents. If your school does not offer something like this, this might be a great project to start. It does not have to be monthly.

Be Proactive

Every school is different. Your child might attend a middle school that is fantastic at communicating or they might not. Do not fall into the trap of blaming the school on its lack of communication and then using that as an excuse for a poor parent/school relationship. If your school does not have the best communication, that can change. The change begins with parents being proactive. Volunteer to start a weekly or even monthly newsletter, updating parents on happenings within the school. Continue to write/call teachers, asking what you can do. Share with other parents. Start a parent group devoted to building school and parent relationships. These are examples of how to be proactive in building relationships with the school.

You also need to be proactive in the individual learning of your child. This does not take a strong relationship with the school, but it does help build a strong relationship with the teacher(s). How can you be proactive in your own child's learning?

- Check your students' grades and assignments regularly on whatever digital platform your child's school uses. I am always surprised to hear parents say, "I do not know how to get into their grades." This is covered at open house or back to school night and information is also sent home. Usually, an educational technologist is available to help. I know every school is different, so if the communication is not coming from the school, then find out how you can access it. It is imperative that you are monitoring your child's grades throughout the quarter, not just at the end. If there are concerns or questions, reach out to the teacher as soon as possible. If you have fostered a relationship with the teacher since the beginning of school, this communication should happen naturally. Ideally, the teacher has been reaching out to you too. Together, you both should be working together to help your child.

- Teach your child to advocate for themselves. Teach them how to address a teacher when they have a question or concern. If you want them to talk to the teacher, practice the scenario at home. Give them sentence starters like:
  - May I please talk to you about my grade. I am concerned because_____.
  - Would you be willing to help me better understand _____? When is a good time to work on this?
  - I have a question about my grades. Is this a good time to talk about them?

- Emphasize the importance of talking to teachers during the quarter, not waiting until the end.

If your child wants to send an email to the teacher, help them draft the letter. At the very least, proofread it. Here is an example of an email I have received: "i finished the assignment. please grade it" If a parent had proofread this email, it would definitely have made a stronger impact. Here is an example of the same email, but with guidance from a parent:

Ms. Wilson,

Thank you for accepting my late assignment on the different types of sentences. I have finished the assignment and submitted it in Google Classroom. Please let me know how I could improve it, after you have had a chance to grade it. Thank you again.

Sincerely,
Bobby

Students need to advocate for themselves, but it often takes adult guidance on knowing how to do this respectfully.

Closing Advice

Building parent-school relationships is crucial in helping your child achieve. Being an active presence in your child's educational experience is so important. It sends a clear message to the school, as well as your child. The middle school years can be challenging for both students and parents. Taking an active role from the beginning lets you have more control in the direction these years go. When schools and parents work together, students are well positioned for academic and social/emotional achievement.

Dos and Don'ts to Building a Parent-School Relationship	
Do	Don't

• Reach out to teachers at the beginning of the year.	• Wait for the school and/or teachers to contact you.
• Continuously reach out to teachers, even when your child seems to be doing well.	• Place blame on the teacher or school personnel.
• Attend school events.	• Assume you know the full story.
• Get involved in school projects or start one of your own.	• Assume your child does not need your involvement.
• Help your child advocate for themselves.	• Assume your child can handle every situation independently.
• Practice how to address a teacher when a concern arises.	• Bad mouth the teachers and/or school within the community.
• Draft or proofread emails that are sent to teachers.	• Post grievances online.
• Speak positively about the school in front of your child.	• Email or talk to teachers only when something is wrong
• Be open-minded.	• Forget we are all on the same team!
• Send affirmations to teachers and school personnel throughout the year.	

Chapter 11
ONLINE DAZE

How can parents best support their virtual student?

Tom Jenkins
2021 Ohio Teacher of the Year Finalist

While the 21st century classroom has always been very dynamic, the COVID-19 pandemic certainly accelerated the technological expectations of both students and teachers. Circumstances demanded that parents become increasingly involved, as learning shifted from the classroom to the home. As a veteran teacher and the parent of a middle school student, I would like to share ways in which parents can enhance home learning. I will share common digital tools that educators use to connect with their students and offer information about how parents and guardians can help their kids outside of the classroom. And I provide tips and conversation starters that may help your student have a more successful middle school academic experience. Of course, while I include suggestions for specific software and websites, it is important that parents use their own judgment about the software that best suits their needs.

Learning from Home

Even though most students are back to in-person learning, it might be nice to hold onto a good setup for remote learning should the need arise. While lack of available space may be a constraint, it is important to create a learning environment that is conducive to remote learning. If a student is in a regularly dedicated working space, they are more likely to pay attention, stay on task, and complete virtual assignments. Care needs to be taken to create an area that is free from distractions, has access to electricity and a strong internet signal, and has a desk-type space where students can complete their work.

Appropriate Technology

Planning for the appropriate technology is something that should also be considered. While it is possible for students to join a remotely taught class using a smartphone, many students perform at higher levels when they have access to a computer, as it has a larger screen and is also equipped with a keyboard. While some school districts have a one student to one computer ratio, the majority do not. Other school districts have computers that are available to borrow, so don't be afraid to ask.

Another option is to purchase a computer for your student. While some computers can cost thousands of dollars or more, many students are used to working on Chromebooks or other smaller portable computers. These can be purchased for less than $300, so having a dedicated machine may be a realistic option. While there are many things to consider when shopping for a computer for online learning, I have listed a few that I took into consideration when purchasing a laptop for my own child:

- Does it have a webcam?
- Does it have integrated speakers and a microphone?

- Does the student require a larger screen or external speakers to be able to see or hear clearly?
- Does the student have classes that necessitate upgraded technical requirements?
- Would the addition of a combination printer/scanner be helpful?

Productivity Software

While many educator-used applications are web-based (meaning they will not require the downloading of software), families may want to have a discussion regarding how the student uses the computer and if any software needs to be added to the machine. Generally, the computer will perform more efficiently if it has a moderate amount of free memory, so it may be necessary to monitor and also limit downloads. However, some applications can be very useful and worth sacrificing some of that space.

A productivity suite like Microsoft Office will allow students to write essays, fill out spreadsheets, prepare presentations, and save files directly to the computer with or without the internet. This software can complement the often-used Google online office suite. It will also allow students to easily download and interact with many different file types.

Many files that are shared between the teacher and the student will take the form of a portable document format, or PDF. This format helps ensure files can easily be transferred as well as read across platforms and software types. Most productivity software allows the user to save as a PDF file, and a PDF reader, such as Adobe Acrobat Reader, should be downloaded to ensure that your student can open this type of document.

Online Learning Platforms

Now that things are set up at home, let's look at ways in which some teachers are managing their online classrooms. The past couple of years have caused even many tech-savvy educators to make a radical shift as they adapt and use more technology to enhance learning opportunities for their students for both in-school and remote learning.

A common online learning platform is Google Classroom. In this virtual space, a teacher can communicate with individual students; create class announcements; moderate group discussions; disseminate relevant course information; and share, receive, and grade assignments. Essentially this can become a class outside of the classroom or even one that is used in tandem with a traditional classroom.

The majority of these online communities are set up as closed environments, where only people from the same organization are permitted to be part of the group. When the teacher provides a class code, only the student will be able to join the class, as this helps to keep the space secure.

Parents and guardians may also have the option to sign up for classroom announcements about their child's academic performance. If this is not available, you can review directly with your child while they are logged into their student account. Not only does this allow full transparency on the child's progress, but it also creates an opportunity for dialogue about the assignment and the course overall.

The tasks assigned by the teacher can take many forms, such as worksheets, web-linked "webquests," presentations, videos, videoconferences, etc. Fortunately, many of these assignments can be completed entirely online, from the creation or download of a document all the way through completion and submission. A calendar can also be linked to keep track of due dates and missing work. Grading and feedback may be provided by the instructor. Many platforms are accessible on a wide range of mobile devices, in addition to personal computers.

Communication

Many districts will set up an email account for their students that they will use to communicate with both their teachers and classmates. It may also allow them to receive updates on school assignments, events, and opportunities. Some teachers may require that assignments be submitted via email, so it can be useful to help your student practice how to send attachments with an appropriate title in the subject line, prior to the start of the school year.

If this is their first email account, it is helpful to have a conversation explaining that they should not use their school email to sign up for games or other apps not related to school. As a teacher who often helps students reset their accounts, I can attest to the fact that many students have an enormous amount of non-school related email. This can lead to disorganization, which may have a negative impact on their grades. Consider setting up a secondary email with your student that can be used to sign up for games and other non-school-related communications, thus freeing up their school account exclusively for academics.

You may also want to consider having a school-related personal email. This will allow you to create an easily identifiable address that can be used to sign up for things like announcements from online learning modules, communicate with teachers, and sign up for applications that will allow you to "stay in the loop." Don't be afraid to ask teachers if you can subscribe to regularly scheduled emails that are sent out by the teachers, school administrators, or district.

Many educators will use a communication application like Remind that allows them to use their phone to communicate with both students and parents without exchanging phone numbers. This program is widely used and can be accessed with a special code provided by the teacher or coach. I often use Remind to share important information involving assignment due dates, upcoming tests, extracurricular activities, and field trips.

Communication Etiquette

It has become typical for a student who enters middle school to have more online responsibilities. Unfortunately, there are times when instructors forget to spend time sharing well-defined expectations regarding their behavior when writing emails and while participating in online discussions. As a parent, I chose to have a conversation with my son regarding things he typed in school-related ecosystems. Below were some of my suggestions:

- Remember that school rules apply whether you are in a school building or working from home. Do not use any word or combination of words that you would not say aloud in class, as it could trigger the school's inappropriate language filter and get you in trouble.
- If you don't know the meaning of a word, do not use it.
- Avoid statements or phrases (even if joking) that could be misconstrued or taken out of context in a negative way.
- Texting slang and abbreviations is inappropriate in a school setting.
- When engaging in a written discussion online, stay on topic and avoid sidebar conversations with classmates.
- Always use the teacher's appropriate formal title/name and always say thank you when sending a direct message.
- Understand that the vast majority of educators take their jobs very seriously and want to help all of their students,

but they also have other students and lives outside of school. They may not immediately reply to messages sent during non-school hours.

Video Conferencing

As school districts have started to provide teachers with better equipment and those same teachers have become more comfortable using different types of technology, video conferencing has become more common. While asynchronous assignments have their place in virtual education, face-to-face interactions with students are indispensable when trying to ensure that a student comprehends the subject matter. That's why it is very important that when students come into a video conference they are prepared to learn.

Just like other facets of parenting, an adult can help increase their child's chances of success by reviewing positive behaviors. Below is a list of helpful video-conferencing tips from my experience as both a parent and a teacher:

- Set up: make sure the room is well lit and free from distractions. Backgrounds should be neutral and free from movement. Virtual backgrounds may also be an option. Ensure that the hardware, software, and internet are functioning properly. Arrive early to the meeting to test the microphone as well as the speakers. Headphones may also help the student focus.
- School dress code should be followed.
- Most of the time, students are not allowed to eat or chew gum during class. The same expectation generally holds for a conference call.

- Try to arrive early or at least be on time. If a student is late, they will either miss part of the call, necessitating a make-up session, or will cause the rest of the class to wait.

- The student's real name should be used when in a virtual classroom setting. Using a different name or a nickname can cause distraction or confusion, especially if the student has the video set to the "off" position.

- Video should be set to the "on" position whenever possible. When teachers are working with students, we often use facial expressions as well as body language to help us communicate with our students. Eye contact with the camera is important.

- Hosts of video conferences will generally "mute" all in attendance until appropriate discussion times. If not, please stress the importance of turning off the microphone when not speaking. Active sound throughout a call can lead to a large amount of distracting noise, including feedback. If a student should desire to speak, they should raise their virtual hand and type a note into the chat portion of the screen.

- When appropriate, type discussion-related questions into the chat box.

- Avoid multitasking while on a call (including texting).

In short, if a student is going to experience growth during a video chat session, then they need to treat it like they are in their actual class. Failure to do so will decrease the chances of academic success.

Online Gradebooks

While many online learning platforms offer grading, many educators use a stand-alone web-based grading program like Progress Book. This type of grading software is an amazing tool for teachers, parents, and students, as it provides a transparent method of sharing grades. After entering a secure code that can be provided by the school office or the educator, both the parent and child can see the scores of all of the assignments that have been posted and shared from either a computer or a mobile device. It is important to note that if the scores in the visible gradebook don't equal the cumulative grade percentage, the teacher has likely marked an assignment, but hasn't "shared" it with the account holders. This is normal, but if the grade doesn't update, an email to the instructor is recommended. Many programs also contain a direct link to a teacher's email account, making communication very easy.

As a parent, I chose to use this type of shared access as a growth opportunity for my son. I downloaded the application on both my phone and my son's phone. I also made sure that both accounts were set up to receive notifications whenever a teacher marked an assignment "missing." This real-time shared information, as well as the consequences at home that went along with the notifications, helped ensure that missing assignments were a rare occurrence. When my son's grade was lower than expected in math, I was able to see that it was primarily a consequence of a low test score, which provided an opportunity for the two of us to sit down and discuss and modify how he prepared for tests.

Education Assessment/Review Games

Studying for tests may never be as fun as playing video games with friends, but I find online educational gaming platforms to be a useful tool for my students. There are a wide variety of games that can either be created from scratch or found in virtual public libraries within websites like Kahoot, Gimkit, and Quizlet that can be used to present test material for review in a fun, low-stress environment. Students can use Chromebooks or their mobile devices to log in and review on their own or in a competitive atmosphere against their peers in the classroom or at home. Data can be collected throughout the game so that strengths and weaknesses can be tracked and later remedied.

Behavioral Management Systems

In most places, phone calls as well as emails home are still a primary way of sharing behavior concerns from school. However, the way that many districts are attempting to influence their students' behaviors is evolving. Applications such as PBIS (Positive Behavioral Interventions and Supports) are pushing beyond sharing only negative reactions and intervention strategies to also highlighting positive student behaviors with both students and parents. Instant notifications allow all parties to not only see when a referral for negative behaviors has been assigned, but also when school staff have recognized something good during the day.

Social Media

Negative interactions between students at school due to posts on social media are becoming increasingly prevalent, forcing administrators to intervene. Even when created at home, controversial posts or those directed at classmates can cause issues at school. These can not only disrupt the normal school day but may also have a negative impact on extracurricular activities. It is important to talk with your child about appropriate and inappropriate behavior on social media.

While there are pitfalls to social media, both parents and students may find value in following their teachers' social media feeds. Many teachers (myself included) regularly post classroom updates on Facebook, Instagram, TikTok, and Twitter. While these updates are rarely essential, they are a good, and often fun, way to share projects, engineering design challenges, performances, and field trips.

Closing Advice: Useful Academic Apps

Below is a list of useful applications recommended by me and my colleagues from other subject areas in the building. While these tools are often used with middle school students, younger and older students may also benefit from their use. There are many similar apps available for download and, as always, I encourage parents to choose the software that suits their needs.

- **Speech to Text**

    Speechnotes is a wonderful web-based way for students to take notes or dictate rough drafts for formal writing assignments. After the audio is transcribed, the keyboard can be used to correct errors, add punctuation, or continue typing the paper. The final draft can then be easily transferred to the type of document the instructor prefers.

- **Math & Science Interactive Simulations**

    ExploreLearning Gizmos and PhET from the University of Colorado are outstanding tools to allow students to explore science topics or mathematical concepts in a meaningful way. These interactive exercises are often standards-aligned and allow student to manipulate variables to achieve a desired outcome or work through various scenarios.

- **Math Tools**

    In my school, Desmos is still used primarily as an online calculator, which is great for dealing with graphing and scientific notation. It is also used by educators for its free digital classroom activities and is helpful when preparing for assessments.

Measure is a free app that can turn a smartphone into a tape measure. While it may not be 100% precise, I have been impressed with its accuracy. It is convenient to have in my pocket. Being able to save photos with measurements is an added plus.

Photomath is an app that all parents and guardians should be aware of. This software is not only able to read and solve math problems, but it can also show the work! The consensus in my building is that it is a wonderful tool if it is used to help the learner and not to do all of the work for them. Many parents use it as a tool to expedite checking their child's homework.

- **Reading**

ThinkFluency is an app that middle school teachers frequently use to assess student reading fluency levels. This and similar apps are preloaded with a wide range of reading prompts and may even allow the user to upload their own. They can measure words read per minute and keep track of errors. ThinkFluency is often recommended by our English as a Second Language (ELA) department as a tool to help students improve their reading proficiency from home.

Newsela may be used in a variety of classrooms to assign relevant standards-aligned news articles. CommonLit is used to provide curated texts as well as student-friendly tools to help increase levels of reading comprehension.

- **Writing**

Formal writing is emphasized in many schools when students reach 7th grade. The Purdue Online Writing Lab is a wonderful free resource for grammar and mechanics and offers many other resources, including those for ESL students.

Citation Machine not only helps you navigate through multiple citation formats, but also assists with sentence structure and writing style. It can also point out areas of unintentional plagiarism found in the writing sample.

> **Conversation Starters**
>
> - What can we improve about your dedicated schoolwork space at home?
> - What word-processing software would benefit your at-home computer or school laptop?
> - Can you show me how you use your online learning platform (i.e., Google Classroom)?
> - What is your school-assigned email address? Do you use it to contact your teachers when you have questions?
> - Can you show me how you access your assignment grades and average online?
> - What education games does your teacher(s) use? What's your favorite and why?
> - Are you aware that your school can see your social media accounts and monitor what you post?

Chapter 12
OUT OF SCHOOL

What should a parent do if a child must miss school?

Erin McCarthy
2020 Wisconsin Teacher of the Year

Missing school days creates a chaotic mix of feelings for middle schoolers. They may feel free and unencumbered by a bell schedule but anxious about missing out on socializing with friends. Even one missed day is a break from their norm and can be disorienting. When my students wrote about their time away from school during the pandemic shutdown of spring 2020, they described emotions ranging from fun to fear, boredom to depression, and anxiety to relaxation. Uncertainty about boundaries felt like freedom at first but quickly turned to worry.

Pandemic learning from home taught families and teachers many valuable lessons. As we tackle what parents should do if a child must miss school, we know a focus on social and emotional well-being is critical. In my 11 years as a middle school teacher and 7 years as a middle-school parent, I've learned that where many students run into trouble is transitioning back to the school routine. Missing assignments and assessments and struggling to master content can create anxiety and leave even the best students overwhelmed. The good news is that living, learning, and adapting through the COVID-19 pandemic made many children and their families aware of the opportunities and pitfalls of learning away from the classroom. Teachers also improved their understanding of the essential elements to help students progress outside of school. Communication is of utmost importance from all three parties—family, students, and teachers.

Plan Ahead for Success

Before planning for a school absence, lay the groundwork for organization. Many systems are available, from paper planners to digital calendars and apps. Having a system for tracking assignments is critical from the start of middle school and will serve your child well when they miss a school day.

After organization, communication is vital. The questions teachers need you to answer to plan for your child's time outside the classroom are:

- How long will the absence be?
- Why will your child be missing school?
- What will be the limitations for learning, and what are the opportunities?
- What is your goal for your child during their absence? (Answers will range from keeping up with the pace of the class to focusing on the experience of a vacation and catching up after they return to healing from surgery while keeping their mind active with some schoolwork, etc.)
- What would be the ideal situation for your child to keep moving forward with learning while they are absent?

Transparency: The Foundation of Cooperation

The second and third questions are essential to address first. Families are entitled to their privacy, but more often than not, little information is shared with classroom teachers. You know your child best and understand what a reasonable workload will be outside the classroom. If your child is recovering from surgery, they may need a vastly scaled-back workload. If your family is traveling to another country for an extended period and quality internet access is unlikely, teachers need time to prepare materials. Be clear about what learning tools will be accessible. For example, reading from a cell phone may work, but completing a worksheet or interactive module may be an exercise in frustration.

Share what you can about the situation directly with teachers when possible. Empathy from teachers will make the absence go smoothly, so help them understand your circumstances with an email. Continued communication ensures that your family, your child, and the team of teachers are just that, a team, all supporting your child's growth as a student and well-being as a teenager.

Honesty about missed days

Be clear about the length of the absence. This point probably seems the most obvious. However, it is essential to set a goal with your child. Every teacher's goal when a child is absent should be for them to continue to make progress and master essential skills without adding anxiety to the child's school experience.

Goals and Priorities as a Proactive Team

Ask teachers about how to prioritize work. I often don't hear about a student missing a week of school until the day before they leave when they ask me to sign a form or ask if there is "anything they will miss." Few things frustrate an educator as much as this conversation.

We think far ahead about our learning goals for our students, but we also make frequent pivots throughout the school week, and even throughout the day, to adapt instruction based on the learners in our classroom. Asking for work in advance is not a simple task with a five-minute turnaround. So, how can you, as a parent or guardian, avoid the tension of this scenario? Be proactive.

1. Be clear about what you need from teachers.
    a. If you will have no access to the internet, do you need photocopies of assignments?
    b. If this is an extended absence, do you need copies of textbooks or other reading materials at home?
2. Clarify who is on your child's support team.
    a. If you are traveling, who will check up on work completion?
    b. If your child is recovering from illness or surgery, who will be with them to help keep up with schoolwork?
    c. How will you or your child ask for help when needed?
    d. Will a video chat enable your child to ask questions?
    e. Is there a classmate who could help keep your child connected to school?
3. Notify classroom teachers, not just the attendance office, of a potential absence with as much notice as you can.
    a. Having time to talk to your child about what they feel they can accomplish when they aren't in school is invaluable to a teacher and ultimately should be the priority for a middle school absence.

4. Extend grace and practice empathy for your child's teachers. In addition to adapting for your child's absence, teachers continue to plan and grade for all students. When your child completes late work, it will take time to grade, provide feedback, and update the grade book.

Empower Your Child: Model Honest Communication

Let's talk about your child's role in their absence. Middle school is a time of transition. As middle school teachers, we know organization, time management, and diligence are rarely the top priorities of a student. We build relationships in the classroom to understand which children need a little extra nudge to get started and who may need frequent redirection. We also know the students riddled with self-doubt and those who push themselves towards perfectionism.

In an ideal world, the process for preparing for a three-day or more absence would look like this:

1. A parent or guardian emails teachers with the facts at least one week before the absence. When? How long? What is your goal for your child? Who will support your child? What are the biggest challenges to progress?

2. Your child emails their teachers at least one week before their absence, if possible, and asks for time to talk to them about when they will be away from school. (This gives teacher and student a chance to plan together, so the right amount of work is assigned.)

3. During the meeting with the teacher, your child talks about how they are progressing, establishes the learning goal when they return to school, and makes a list of:

- Work they will miss in class.

- Assessments they will need to complete in advance or when they return.
- What they should do when they are away from school.
- What they should do when they return.

Then your child should share how they feel about the absence. How do they feel about the plan the teacher has shared? Do they feel confident and prepared to be successful? Finally, your child and their teachers set a time to meet after your child returns to check in again. They put this date on a calendar.

When Your Child Returns

Returning to school after an absence of more than a day is a critical transition time that is often overlooked. As adults, we often forget how a middle school brain works. Imagine taking a week's vacation from work and missing important meetings and calls from clients. Upon returning, you get to work as if you never left. You catch up with your colleagues, but you don't address anything work-related that happened during your time off. You don't return phone calls from anyone who left you a voicemail or respond to any emails. You don't ask what happened at meetings you missed. This is the middle schooler's approach to missing school. For most middle schoolers, the social aspect of school is an essential element of their day. Reconnecting with their friends and classmates will be their priority when they return to school. But imagine how your supervisor or boss would react if you failed to address deadlines and important work missed in your absence. Teachers feel this frustration and disappointment when students return and fail to follow up.

As a parent of three teenagers, I understand entirely the desire to give them the freedom to learn from their mistakes. We believe they will get caught up and talk to teachers about things they missed, but this level of responsibility is the exception and not the rule, especially in 7th grade. You can, however, set your child up for success by including them in the follow-up process. This is an important time to teach self-advocacy. Your child missed instruction; therefore, they must ask questions in class and for additional tools and resources to understand what they missed.

Responsibility as Follow-up

After your child returns to school, model responsibility for them; please do not wait for a crisis moment, like a failed grade or a breakdown from your upset child.

1. Talk about the transition back to school and ways to keep anxiety and stress at bay.
2. Think of this time as transitional. There might be a little more homework to get back on track, but it won't last for long.
3. Look at the online grade book with your child. Talk about assignments that have been marked missing.
4. What is the plan to make up missed assignments, notes, instructions, and in-class learning experiences?
5. Discuss who could help them complete missing work.
6. Communicate with teachers. Ask your child to write an email to a teacher that focuses on completing work or prioritizing assignments. Together, propose a plan to get back on track.
7. Proofread this email together before sending it and ask your child to copy you on the email.

The final step is to consistently check in on your child's progress. Show them how to have empathy for their teacher, who will need time to mark their work and update their grade book. A positive attitude and patience will go a long way towards keeping stress at bay.

Scenarios to Consider

Three things to think about for family vacations

Vacation is a time to rest and recharge. Children need to see you modeling self-care and work-life balance. If you must vacation outside of scheduled school break times:

1. **Think about your goal:** If your goal is for your child to not miss out on any content and stay on pace with peers in the classroom despite missing a week of in-person instruction, your expectations are not realistic. Your child will fall behind in some subjects and not have the same depth of understanding.

2. **Model planning for downtime:** Help your child communicate in advance so they can work ahead in some subjects and make use of rest during travel (planes, car rides, etc.) to get work done.

3. **Be realistic about support:** After returning, help your child make a schedule to get caught up. Help them contact teachers and put reminders on a calendar to ask for help or complete missing work as needed.

Three things to consider about medical absences (planned)

1. **Think about your goal:** No teacher wants to add to a child's fear and anxiety, so advocate for your child and be honest about realistic goals. Mental and physical health are top priorities, and as teachers, we want to extend grace to keep your child well.

2. **Model reflection:** This is an excellent opportunity for your child to be honest with you about which classes they feel confident in and where they need a little more support. We all could use this kind of reflection in our lives.

3. **Be realistic about help:** A buddy system is a classic tool used by teachers to support students. Ask your child about classmates they could rely on to share notes or bring them missing work. Alternatively, would a video chat with a teacher be a good idea? Would a tutor help your child stay on track in the short or long term?

Two things to consider about medical absence (unplanned)

1. **Think about your goal:** Wellness is most important. Please let your child return to total health before sending them back to school.

2. **Model communication:** Help your child write an email to their teachers asking for support. This email can be as short and as simple as: "I missed a week of class because I was sick, and I'd like your help coming up with a plan to get caught up. Can we meet on Monday after school?"

Closing Advice

The list of scenarios could stretch on indefinitely, as we live in a world of endless possibilities. As I write this chapter, my children are missing five months of in-person school while I conduct research in Greece. I'm teaching them to set goals and to recognize their limitations, but we still struggle at times. While our situation allows for many opportunities to learn beyond their virtual classes, they still need to be realistic about returning to desks in classrooms. We are dealing with frustrations and finding creative ways to solve problems. All of this informs the advice in this chapter. My team back at my middle school also helped craft the advice here. As middle school teachers, we help students see connections between what they are doing and their future. Being a clear communicator who sets goals and takes responsibility is essential for success in the real world. We can help middle schoolers practice this every day, especially when they miss school.

> ### Conversation Starters
>
> - Which classes do you feel most anxious about missing in-person learning?
> - Which classmates could you ask to share notes with or to stay connected with school during your absence?
> - When will you be sitting down with your teacher(s) to come up with a plan (either before or after) your absence to keep up with schoolwork?
> - Tell me about the plan you came up with together; do you feel confident and prepared?
> - Who could help you complete any missing assignments?
> - What kinds of projects or assessments will you be working on to get caught up when you are back in school?

Chapter 13
FINDING PASSIONS IN AND OUT OF SCHOOL

How to discover and support your
child's interests and activities

Meghan Everette
2013 Alabama Teacher of the Year Finalist

Middle school is a time of change for children. As they make the move from childhood to the teen years, their brains and bodies are rapidly developing. For kids to become active, engaged teens and young adults, they need to follow their passions and be supported in discovering themselves and any opportunities that interest them. Few 7th graders are confident about their own interests, and those that are often have a limited outlook on what is available to them. At the same time, it can be challenging for parents to connect student interests to activities, help prioritize and plan events, and navigate their children's changing selves. This chapter helps parents investigate interests, provide support, find balance, and know when to quit.

Identifying an Interest

By middle school, some kids will have activities that they have participated in for years while others will be engaging in extracurricular groups for the first time. No matter if your child is already hyper-involved, thinking about trying something new, or is seemingly uninterested in anything, the most important thing a parent can do is listen to their child. Notice I didn't say *talk* to their child. Why? Parents inadvertently steer conversations and even seemingly innocuous suggestions can shut down discussion with teens. While some kids respond well to pointed questions, listening and watching over time gives more information. For kids still struggling to know themselves, pointed questions may cause anxiety. A child who wants to satisfy their parents might try to guess at what will make their family happy. A confused child may become angry or tearful. And an oppositional child may not answer at all. How can a parent find out what might interest their child if they don't sit down and have a direct conversation? Try these approaches:

Watch

You probably notice things about your child that could generate ideas about their interests and feelings without ever realizing it. For example, does your child take time to cultivate their "look," including clothing, hair, or makeup? Or do they spend hours watching content creators on social media? Are your kids asking to watch a certain type of movie or always listening to a particular musician? Do they bury their noses in books? Does your child seem to connect better with your pets than with other people? All of these interests can connect to potential activities. Understanding what excites your child can sometimes be as simple as watching what they are already doing with intention. Some parents say their child does "nothing," but when they stop and watch, they can identify activities the kid engages in. It just might not be something the family deems "productive," such as watching TV.

Listen

What are you listening for? Listen for what your child brings up. When you ask about school, friends, or activities, what are they most likely to give details about? When does your child seem the most animated and excited? Even if they can't describe exactly what they want to do, they can probably give you some hints about what excites them. Don't discount interests that you aren't sure relate to an activity. If your child is interested in video games, nature, clothes, makeup, social media, board games…no matter the topic, listen to what gets them excited.

Question

You don't have to sit down and have an official "talk" with your child. As mentioned, many young people aren't comfortable with that kind of direct questioning and even those who want to give you an answer may not know themselves well enough to articulate their thoughts. Instead, ask questions that let them explain their interests. Be sure that any questions sound like a genuine attempt at understanding, rather than an accusation. Offer opportunities for them to show you what they are doing and let them lead. Ask questions that show you appreciate that their interest is important to them.

The Trouble with Questions

Even loving families with great relationships find themselves in the minefield that is questioning a 7th grader. These early teens are changing rapidly and sometimes can't explain their own apathy, interest, or shifting needs. Anyone who has spent time with a teen knows they are masters of misconstruing what you are saying. Why? This is an age that struggles with identity. They are often unsure and self-conscious, so they assume others are seeing the faults and uncertainty they feel themselves. A few 7th graders do remain blissfully unaware of these changes, and it may seem as though they don't take anything too seriously. What it means for adults trying to engage children is that conversations require intentionality.

Example: Your child has been watching a content creator online.

Question: What are you watching? Why do you like that?

What They Hear: That isn't interesting or important, so why are you doing it?

What You Really Want to Know: What is it about this content or creator that is interesting?

A Better Approach: Start with something you notice or make a connection. Try something like "I like how that guy's voice sounds…what does he create content about?" or "Is that the girl that makes cat videos? I wonder how she got started." Once a safe entry point is established, you can ask to see the best video or example, or ask which segment is their favorite. It's also important not to react in the moment if you hear something objectionable. You can always bring it up later, but right now you want to find out what it is that has captured your child's attention.

Example: Your child doesn't want to go to something they have participated in for years, such as soccer practice or piano lessons.

Question: Why aren't you practicing?

What They Hear: What is wrong with you?

A Better Approach: You are trying to determine if your child is having self-doubts, if there's something wrong at practice, or if they are simply losing interest in childhood activities. It's important to keep in mind that a pre-teen might not know exactly why their interest is changing, only that it is. As long as you don't suspect any kind of abuse or bullying, you might try approaching the situation with an end in mind. Your conversation might sound like, "we committed to your team for this season but sign up for next season starts in May. I've noticed you don't seem to enjoy practice. How are you feeling about signing up for next year?" You can also discuss what they enjoy about an activity and what might feel challenging. You could say, "I know soccer seems hard for you right now. Are there things you feel proud of or enjoy about the sport still? Is there a way I can help you?"

Example: Your child doesn't seem to be interested in anything.

Question: Why don't you do something?

What They Hear: You are lazy, a loner, a loser, and boring.

A Better Approach: After trying the "watch" strategy mentioned earlier in this chapter, approach your child with some options. It's important that they know you are giving a few broad starting points and not forcing a decision right now. This might sound something like, "I want to support you to do some kind of activity. It's okay with me if it is academic, sports, arts, competitive, or not... I am open to things I don't know anything about as long as you are interested." It's also helpful to put a decision timeline out for them: "Here are a few things I thought you might be interested in... Take a look and let's talk about them next weekend. I would like to sign you up for something for the summer session. If you end up not liking it, we can find something else to try next year."

What do you do when a conversation goes wrong? Be direct and then give time and space. You might try something like, "I can see that I've upset you. I did not mean to. I'd like to talk to you about this later this week. I hope you feel like you can share your feelings with me." Kids need to hear that you care, you are not intentionally hurting them, and you will revisit the conversation. If you can tell them what you'd like to know and then let them think about it, they might be able to share a response after taking some time to think. It might look like they are shut off, angry, sad, or not going to respond, but often they just need more time to reflect and formulate a response. Above all, make sure they know you are not disappointed in them, but just wanting to support them in trying new things.

Understanding and Connecting

Sometimes kids come up with interests and activities that don't make much sense to adults. Maybe parents or older siblings have been involved in activities that are different from what is interesting to the child. Maybe parents were musicians, but their child wants to be an athlete. Perhaps parents were readers or into computers while their child wants to be an artist. This is compounded when activities are even less traditional.

> ### Real Life Example
>
> My son has played soccer since he was two. It was part of his identity and when we moved to a new state, he was immediately welcomed by a new team. In 7th grade, he asked me to take him to an Ultimate Frisbee practice for the middle school players as part of the high school team. It didn't seem particularly official, and practice was at a local park. I didn't see uniforms and I didn't understand the sport, but I told him I could get

> him to practice if he could get me an adult to talk to. After a season with the team, he decided to quit soccer and focus on Ultimate. We talked about his personal identity, which had been so wrapped up in soccer, and how he would feel not be a "soccer kid" anymore. I was also worried that Ultimate wouldn't provide the same kind of competition—something he had always enjoyed. But he not only found a great group of friends with Ultimate, he is happier and healthier than ever. Last year, he joined the state team and won a national championship in the sport. It was scary to watch him give up a sport that we knew and understood, but his new sport keeps him mentally and physically challenged without some of the pressures soccer was putting on him. I'm glad I listened and helped him get to that first practice.

What happens when your child's interest doesn't seem to connect to an organized activity? Honor that their interest might be something they do alone, and that's okay. Consider how you can take that interest and connect it to the school, community, or world. Can your child write, blog, vlog, podcast, or share their interest in some other way? Is there a way for them to get feedback or connect with people interested in the same things they are? Check the library; the local book, comic, or coffee shops; and online meetup sites. With safe boundaries, kids can create and publish content or connect to groups online. Think about the advocacy that might interest your child and encourage them to be involved.

Look for adjacent activities too, those that are related to your child's primary interest but that might not seem immediately obvious. For example, a child who is into reading might find connection in a book club. An adjacent interest might be joining a 'zine teen group at the library, writing online reviews, or reading aloud to younger students. They might even write a book study guide for others. A child who is into watching YouTube might want to create how-to videos on something they feel confident about, from math problems to makeup to stop-motion art. These adjacent activities aren't just great for children looking to do something new. They can also add a new dimension and bring back passion for activities when they start to feel stale or boring.

Support

I spoke to a group of 7th graders that were involved in a variety of activities (from Magic: The Gathering club to youth orchestra to travel baseball) and asked them what their parents did to help them get, and stay, involved. None of them were able to express exactly what their families did, but it all came down to patience and support. While a few mentioned covering the cost of activities, they were quicker to mention giving rides to practice, washing uniforms, and helping them coordinate schedules.

On finances: most 7th graders recognize that their activities cost money and are able to understand basic family finances. There are a variety of ways to pay for activities. Most groups offer scholarships and payment plans. Students can do small jobs, such as lawn mowing or babysitting, or organize fundraising to offset costs. Some groups provide discounts in exchange for parent help with registration, social media, or a snack shack. You might help others in need by organizing a uniform or gear exchange. Special supplies could be wrapped up with birthday or holiday gifts. Also, pace your investment. It might seem like *every* player has a new gear bag, but is it necessary to play? Probably not. Talk to the group manager and find out what is indispensable. No matter what, consider holding off on major investments until your child is a bit older.

> **Real Life Example**
>
> Oboes are instruments made from temperamental wood that requires special care and they are very expensive. When I joined the school band, we borrowed a plastic version from my school to take home to practice. After I moved to a new school with a bigger band program, the band director suggested renting a student oboe. By high school, my family purchased a student oboe but it was only when I started looking into college music programs that my parents helped me invest in a professional instrument.

Don't confuse support with blind commitment. As students grow, they are faced with many competing priorities. Sometimes even before 7th grade, students find family, faith, and friends fighting for limited time and resources. One way parents can avoid overcommitment and maintain balance is to discuss priorities. Parents need to decide what is most important to the family and consistently reinforce expectations. For example, if school is a top priority for your family, then discuss your expectations about not missing class for activities or about completing homework before evening or weekend obligations.

Finally, there are children in the world who will become world-class musicians, athletes, or internet stars, but they will need solid communication, collaboration, and academic skills. Consider that only about 7% of high school football players play in college and in 2019, only 0.102% of high participants made it to the NFL, according to the NCAA's 2020 report, "Football: Probability of Competing beyond High School." Other sports, such as basketball, have even lower rates. Now consider how many professional football players or world-class pianists you know. The point is, your child might be one of those lucky few who has exceptional talent, opportunity, and luck aligned, but the chances are more likely that they will be well-rounded, educated citizens, so let them explore all the options and enjoy the journey with them.

Commitment and Priorities

One of the best skills students learn from engaging in activities inside or outside of school is commitment. There is a responsibility to the group, much like the commitment parents make to their jobs or community groups. Students are changing rapidly at this age, and they might become disenchanted with an activity they decided to try (or maybe even one they have loved for a long time.) What do you do when your child wants to quit? Ask yourself these questions:

- Is the stress caused by the activity manageable? If not, is the activity worth the potential cost to mental health?
- Is the reason your child wants to quit going to go away when the activity ends, or is there something else going on (such as anxiety or self-doubt that might benefit from mental health care)?
- Is there an end date? (It can be beneficial for kids to see a light at the end of the tunnel. Also, knowing they can revisit the option to quit at the end of a season or session can be useful.)
- Are others depending on them? (Assuming the activity is physically and mentally safe, fulfilling the commitment is a good lesson in responsibility.)
- Are there alternatives? Could another teacher, program, group, or time work better for your child?

> **Real Life Example**
>
> My younger sister was a competitive gymnast. Starting in 2nd grade, she attended conditioning, training, and team events most days every week. She was good and often found herself on the medal stand at local and state meets. By middle school she started not eating the morning of competition and would say she wanted to quit, her body hurt, or her stomach was upset. Eventually, my mom took her to the doctor, and she was diagnosed with ulcers resulting from self-imposed stress. While she was successful, never cried, and had great teachers, she was mentally stretching herself too thin. At the end of the season, she quit, but in high school, she was able to draw on her skills to become color guard captain—an activity she excelled at because of her previous dedication and talent, but which didn't wear on her health.

Closing Advice

One of the best pieces of advice my parents gave me that I have repeated often with my own children and students is, "You have to do *something*, but you can't possibly do *everything*." Balanced listening, support, facilitation, and understanding that align with family priorities and values will serve students now and as they continue to grow.

Chapter 14
ARE THEY READY FOR 8TH GRADE?

Tips, Quips, and Tools

LéAnn Murphy Cassidy
2018 Connecticut History Teacher of the Year and Connecticut Teacher of the Year Finalist

Middle school is kind of like Middle Earth, full of mystery and intrigue, drama and comedy, and loads of "organized chaos" daily. Like the imaginary characters in Tolkien's novels, no such thing as a typical eleven-, twelve-, or even thirteen-year-old exists in middle school. They are as different as night and day in many instances, but in others, they are still the bright-eyed inquisitive children you remember so well from elementary school. The time between 7th and 8th grades can be summed up by my favorite button from yesteryear: "If all the world's a stage, I want better lighting!" It is the time when your child is gaining better insight into themselves, and with that comes their desire for more: more independence, more friends, more successes, and more autonomy in their daily lives.

How does one go about determining their child's capacity to independently plan and monitor their academic and emotional selves when their bodies are wreaking havoc on them both physically and emotionally? Simple: by just letting it be. When we try to force a preset notion of where a child should be by a given grade, we often pigeonhole them into a system that does not work. My five children are now grown, with jobs and lives of their own, but each brought a different skill set to the middle school experience and they all entered high school at varying developmental levels. Each grew in their own time. Looking back, I often wonder how they all became such amazing adults when there were times when I wanted to throttle them as middle schoolers, particularly my youngest. They were moody, defiant, outspoken, belligerent, excited, enthusiastic, beautifully creative, and loving all rolled into one. It is for precisely this reason that I love middle school. There is always something new and exciting to learn, and I get to help children discover as they grow and develop as human beings. There is never a dull moment in middle school!

I find joy in each day because my students are not the same and are not in the same place. It makes discussions exciting. It makes learning fun, and above all else, it allows my students to begin to discover who they hope to become as people. In the age of "helicopter" and "tiger" parenting, I can honestly say that it is often better to push your children out with a parachute of love and support. Middle school is one of the best places to do this. Your children can make mistakes and learn from them without fear of ruining their chances of getting into college or onto a specific career path. Students will be nurtured as they try out new personas and ideas in a supportive environment where risk-taking is expected. Students need to discover that they can manage, are accountable to themselves, and most of all that they have limitless possibilities and abilities.

Is My Child Emotionally Prepared?

Eighth grade is that bridge from youth to young adult. You are beginning to ask if your child is ready for 8th grade. Are they mature enough? Are they emotionally prepared? The answer to all of these questions is a resounding yes! Children develop at their own speed and will come into their own as they traverse 8th grade and continue into high school. My children each found their niche, and their journey to independence began in earnest in 8th grade. Each one developed at their own rate, with love and support from their parental units, who sometimes had to let them pick themselves back up after a struggle.

Having taught 7th and 8th grade for over 25 years, I know that the physical and emotional growth is tremendous during this time. My students will tell you that now, more than ever, they feel the pressure of peers in all things, from clothing choices to work ethic. Peer groups matter. At the outset, the average 7th grader is quite spirited and enthusiastic, is inclined to focus longer than previously able, becomes more focused on self, and then can be downright moody. As they progress through to 8th grade, they learn to get through the melodrama that can be school as they gain more maturity and improve their interpersonal skills. They also begin to find what makes them happy as they try school activities, join teams, and watch friend groups change and evolve. A typical 8th grader wants to belong while also needing to be their own individual. We see it in their clothing, their hair, and the way they carry themselves.

When my children were in 7th grade, they often went from being very independent to very clingy and needy in minutes, depending on the circumstance. Students at this age want to appear independent, but they are still unsure how to make that happen consistently. Gradual release, a strategy that shifts the responsibility from teacher or parent to the child through a series of scaffolded learning activities, works wonders. Students go from needing direct assistance to becoming fiercely independent while adults around them are slowly stepping back. Now is the time to allow them to make missteps, from which they may learn and improve. It encourages the growth of self-confidence and internal motivation, which will impact future successes. I always tell my students that they never fail. It is always a "first attempt in learning." As a history teacher, I generally throw in examples of famous people who have failed repeatedly in their attempts but have persevered in life. Setting high expectations that can be flexible based on individual needs is vitally important at this stage.

Is My Child Academically Prepared?

Good teaching meets children where they are, not where we expect them to be in their development. As parents, you are probably concerned about whether your child is academically ready for 8th grade. You will might get a laundry list of what your child should know and be able to do by the end of 7th grade. It most likely will include:

- Analyze non-fiction texts and use evidence to support a claim.
- Write informative papers using science and social studies vocabulary.
- Support arguments both in writing and in speech.
- Make research-based presentations to one's peers.
- Solve multi-step math problems.
- A host of other standards-based learning outcomes.

Rest assured, if your child cannot do all of these by the start of 8th grade, the work will continue, and your child will still be ready for 8th grade. Your children are individuals, with individual needs that don't all follow the same schedule.

For those of you worried because your child learns differently or has a 504 or an IEP, we've got your child covered. All children learn differently. It is the job of your child's teacher, or teachers, to personalize the educational opportunities so that your child has equitable learning experiences that allow for success. Your child may be behind their peer group based on normed standards for their grade, but that does not mean that they will not be successful in 8th grade and beyond. As both a teacher and a mom, I understand the struggle and the worry.

Middle school was a struggle for my youngest due to his learning disability and ADHD. Did he meet all of the standards for 7th grade before he moved to 8th grade or for 8th before he moved to high school? No, he did not. Did he go on to graduate from college magna cum laude? Yes, he did. Through a long process that included love and support, he learned to access education in a way that made sense to him. Today he is a successful trauma nurse. All children have limitless possibilities. Never underestimate the power of your support and hard work as parents and as team members in the educational process. As a teacher, I never underestimate my students because I learn something wonderful and new about them each day. They are truly magnificent creatures!

Managing Executive Functions and Self-Regulating Emotions

I became a middle school teacher because of my difficult middle school experiences. I loved to learn and was into music and the arts, but I was an exceedingly shy introvert. I also happened to be the shortest person in the school, wore glasses, and sported the horrible orthodontia of old. Sound familiar? Jokes and bullying were part of my existence. Today, we better understand the negative impact this can have on a child. It is why schools work so hard to be inclusive and welcoming for all students. It is also why emphasis is placed on helping children develop problem-solving skills as well as skills of empathy and compassion. Social-emotional growth is a crucial component of middle-level education. In my opinion, behavioral and emotional growth are more important than academic standards at this point in a student's educational career. To quote Aristotle, "Educating the mind without educating the heart is no education at all." Simply put, middle school is a time when your child will experience many emotional changes.

As parents and teachers, we can help children identify their emotions better so that they can self-regulate across different situations that they might encounter as their personal lives become more independent. Middle school can be a daily melodrama. Friend groups go through iterations on a regular basis. Minor misunderstandings can become full-blown dramas and may seem impossible to resolve without first practicing dealing with their personal emotions in difficult situations. Here are some suggestions for helping your child practice this emotional self-regulation:

- Discuss positive ways to manage emotions.
- Talk about stressors and find ways to help your child reduce stress by taking brain breaks, exercising, or playing music.
- Build coping strategies for different types of social situations.
- Encourage your child to find the positives in every day.
- Talk to your child about school each day.

Middle school can be socially and academically daunting. Working to help your child build a positive sense of self goes a long way towards building strong and independent young adults who will be ready for 8th grade and beyond. When they feel heard, validated, and empathized with, children have a better basis for problem-solving as they get older. When you work in tandem with their teachers, your children gain a sense of self and well-being that carries into all aspects of their development.

Many middle school students also struggle in other areas of executive functioning, such as planning and organization, initiating tasks, attending to the task at hand, or managing their time. Adults can help their children by providing them with a consistent place to study free from distractions such as phones, gaming systems, and other media. Encourage them to self-advocate when they are having issues and need to ask for help. Let them do some problem-solving when they encounter academic difficulties. Discuss with your child ways to strengthen their abilities to manage their time with tools such as planners, checklists, timers, and even organization applications on their phones. Mastering these skills will not only benefit them in 8th grade but throughout the rest of their life.

Celebrate and Honor Uniqueness

As your child nears the end of 7th grade, don't be surprised if they begin speaking in one-word sentences or short phrases. It is how they communicate regularly with their closest confidantes. In this age of emojis and Snapchat, middle schoolers are ahead of most parents and teachers in their technological skills. They will be helping you with your IT difficulties. But while technically savvy, students can lack the ability to take learning risks for fear of embarrassing themselves in front of their peers. Many students struggle with their sense of identity and where they fit in, and this might be one of the biggest obstacles you face as a middle school parent. Middle school students often worry about being "normal." Most students can't seem to define what "normal" actually means, which can lead to difficulties with peers and with personal confidence.

When I was a middle schooler in the mid-'70s, my mom had a t-shirt made for me that reads: "I was normal once. I didn't like it." I still have that t-shirt because it reminds me of an essential aspect of middle school: helping children recognize their uniqueness as something to be celebrated and cherished. Reminding children that they are enough and that their voices matter makes all the difference in middle school. They need to know that they are valued and that what they have to say and offer is important. Our hope is that by the time they are ready for 8th grade, they are also prepared to understand and appreciate their individual gifts.

Closing Advice

I liken the summer between 7th and 8th grade to the caterpillar finally turning into a beautiful butterfly. Most children will mature both physically and emotionally. As they enter 8th grade, students begin to accept more responsibility for their academic performance. Those who aren't quite there will realize soon enough that now is the time to put more focus on being their best selves, with the guidance of their teachers. Academically, that will mean completing and turning in assignments on time, accepting responsibility for their work and behavior, choosing peer groups that help them become the best versions of themselves, and actively involving themselves in the school culture. Eighth grade is a time for parents to let go a little more so that each child becomes increasingly independent and learns to become a better self-advocate.

Never fear; your child will survive 8th grade, and so will you. Your child, most likely a teenager by early 8th grade, is on their way to becoming an adult. You will see both the child and the young adult in their sense of wonder and discovery as they continue to grow and change. It will be as exciting as it is exasperating at times. One morning you will wake up and find a more independent, resilient, and engaging human being sitting across the table from you. Encourage them always to be kind, ask questions, read, write, and read some more, but most importantly, tell them to believe in themselves, because they are the future.

Conversation Starters

- Can you tell me some examples of when you've stepped up to be a leader during a group project, presented in front of your classmates, reached out to new friends, or joined a new club at school?
- What peer pressure do you feel at school, if any? How does it make you feel?
- Do you feel like you can be your own individual in what you like to wear or what extracurricular activities you do?
- Is there a lot of melodrama that goes on in school? How do you deal with it?
- Do you feel academically prepared for 8th grade? In what areas or particular subjects could you use some help?
- Do you need any help with organizing your workload or planning for homework and studying? What do you feel would help you best in organizing your time and materials?
- What brings you joy? What motivates you?
- Where in school do you feel most yourself?

www.ingramcontent.com/pod-product-compliance
Lightning Source LLC
Chambersburg PA
CBHW011758040426
42446CB00018B/3450